Why Bureaucracy Fails

Attention Authors

Manas Publications is fighting a war to tell the world that India can win the battle not only by the bullet but also by pen. We are converting fighters into writers. There is no dearth of intellectuals in our country. However, their knowledge is confined to them only. No sincere effort has been made by any other publisher to channelise their knowledge. That is why the talent of every intellectual remains latent. An author always presents the raw material in the shape of a manuscript and it is the job of the publisher to convert it into a completely finished book. Manas has been motivating intellectuals continually and publishing their manuscripts for more than three decades and would like to publish your manuscript too. If you or your colleagues have a manuscript ready for publication or are working on it, contact us with a detailed synopsis and list of contents. Manas can also suggest you a suitable title for writing related to your area of expertise. Manas is known for its publishing quality. We take utmost care in production and give wide publicity to the book and its author through our national and international distribution network.

Why Bureaucracy Fails

Kalyan Ray, IAS

Manas Publications
(We Convert Fighters into Writers)
New Delhi-110002 (INDIA)

MANAS PUBLICATIONS
(Publishers, Library Suppliers, Importers & Exporters)
4402/5-A, Ansari Road (Opp. HDFC Bank)
Darya Ganj, New Delhi-110 002 (INDIA)
Off. © 23260783, 23265523, Res. © 23842660
Fax: 011-23272766
E-mail: manaspublications@vsnl.com
manaspublications@yahoo.com

New Impression 2015

ISBN 978-81-7049-400-3

₹ 695/-

Designed by
Manas Publications

Printed in India at
RK Print Services, Delhi
and published by Mrs Suman Lata for
Manas Publications, 4402/5-A, Ansari Road
(Opp. HDFC Bank),
Darya Ganj, New Delhi-110 002 (INDIA)

To

Swapna

Contents

Preface

This book is not in the nature of an autobiography or a memoir. Of course in writing this book, I have drawn upon my personal experience to a certain extent. As far as possible or practicable, I have tried to take a dispassionate view of men and matters, keeping in view a historical or time perspective of events and the participants.

Something, which appears to us to be of great importance and affects us personally at a particular point of time, looks to be quite commonplace or insignificant after a passage of time. In view of this, a personal upward rising career graph, though highly satisfying to the individual and his immediate family, may not be of great importance in the affairs of an organisation. Upwardly rising individual career graphs do not ensure success of the organisation. This is one of the tragedies of the present day, that in spite of having some of the best products of the educational system, the bureaucracy is languishing. Individual career developments are not the best indicators of the health of the organization. However, there are many developments in the field of public service, which may not appear to be too significant in the immediate present, but have great bearing on the future of the organisation. I have tried to analyse some of these developments, which are likely to have effect on the democratic system of government.

Theories of public administration are mostly country specific, although there may be some elements of commonality. Bureaucracy of a country moulds itself on the societal norms. Bureaucracy is in fact a society in miniature.

If the society is rationalistic, bureaucracy will follow suit and similarly if the society is ritualistic, bureaucracy will also be the same. If the society is egalitarian, bureaucracy will adopt similar social norms and if the society is feudal and hierarchical, bureaucracy will also be the same. Indian society being both ritualistic and hierarchic, Indian bureaucracy has modelled itself on that pattern. In fact the administrative system devised by the British, which we inherited, was to a great extent modelled on the Indian social system.

I have generally used the term 'bureaucracy', as this is the most accepted term in India nowadays and encompasses the entire government system. A term like 'civil service' or 'administrative system' will hardly serve the purpose, to visualise the huge government machinery and its functioning. The term seems to have acquired a sinister and somewhat derogatory tone in recent times and nobody likes to be called a 'bureaucrat'. However, nobody can do without bureaucracy. Even the free market believers, who breathe fire against the 'license, control Raj', cannot do without acquiring land at a low cost through bureaucratic procedure of Land Acquisition Act, while setting up their industries or having the benefit of Special Economic Zone (SEZ). They do not depend on the market forces to purchase land from the land holders. There are numerous such cases, as to persons as well as organizations, which are vehemently against any government interference, have no hesitations in asking for and accepting government largesse. These are some of the paradoxes of the present situation, where the bureaucracy is hardly in a position to please everybody and comes out worse of the bargain.

There is obviously a love-hate relationship of the general citizenry with the bureaucracy. This, to a great extent, is due to the long period of foreign rule, when we were governed, rather than administered. This has also made us forget to rule ourselves and become over dependent on the government system. Centuries of foreign rule has destroyed the self-governing institutions at the local level, which is the basis of a democratic system of government. A paternalistic system of administration, which the British government introduced, where the Big Brother knows the best, has made us somnambulist and over dependent on the administrative system. Basically a society should govern itself. Administration can only act as a catalytic agent.

Before independence, we had little expectations from the administration and whatever services were made available, were generally unquestioningly accepted. Being the administration of the Big Brother, run from thousands of mile away, it had an aura of its own and enjoyed considerable prestige. All these changed after independence and our expectations from the government shot up, little realising that we ourselves have become responsible for meeting the same and administration is only a means to an end. With sky rocketing expectations, we expected the administration to usher in the proverbial Ram Raj. This is of course a utopian concept and is neither possible nor practical. However, long period of foreign rule made us pine for this Ram Raj. This never materialised and various problems of a newly independent country, long impoverished, trying the development process, cropped up. We were beset by serious self doubt, as to whether we are capable of ruling ourselves. We had tried too many things too fast in a semi-feudalistic society, which is yet to get over a fatalistic mindset. With the crisis of expectations, we were in search of scapegoats. Two such were immediately available, in the guise of politicians and bureaucrats.

Politicians, particularly those coming through direct elections and having to face the electorate at short intervals, are the most vulnerable group to accusations of non-performance and corruption. Being the public face of democracy, they are the favourite whipping boys of the so-called intellectuals and the media. It is perhaps little realised that direct elections cost lot of money for the candidates and not having developed legal sources of funding elections, politicians have to resort to shady practices. Elections in the United States of America cost staggering sums of money and are funded by various lobbies and individuals, who expect quid pro quo. But the funding has been systematised and hardly any questions are asked, except when the person becomes inconvenient, as happened in the case of President Nixon. In the United Kingdom, the mother of democracy, only those with huge landed property or sufficient personal income could aspire for a seat in the Parliament, till lately. In India, with full adult franchise, electoral arena was accessible to anybody, prepared to face the electorate. This was not to the liking of many, steeped in feudal mindset.

The accessibility of the common man to the power structure was a major blow to the existing feudal system and vested interests. It was the boldest step in empowering the people, which is talked so much these days. It was not liked by the dominant colonial Western lobby and a canard was started about corruption in the Indian polity. In fact, there is a regular business in the form of various so-called think tanks to show the Indian political system in a bad light. Politicians themselves also become a party to it, as theirs is the only profession, which wash their dirty linen in public. Corruption index and other parameters devised by the Western powers are tendentious and designed to show newly independent countries, particularly India, in a bad light and destroy the faith of the people in democracy. The simple message, they want to register, is Indians are incapable of governing themselves. This refrain has come all the way down from Cornwallis to Churchill, through the British Raj. Unless they have Indians as cheerleaders, they can hardly hope to succeed. This exercise has dangerous overtones and has brought down democracy in many countries, replacing it with military dictatorship.

It speaks of the vibrant nature of the Indian polity, that continuous onslaught by vested interests to shake the faith of the people in the democratic system, has not succeeded. While holding no brief for the corrupt elements, we should not miss the wood for the trees and nothing should be done to weaken the nascent democratic system. While we should be vigilant about political corruption, similar vigilance is not shown in the exposure of various multi-crore scams by public spirited individuals or bodies. These are generally brushed aside as aberrations of market forces. A few, public sector bureaucrats, who offer soft targets, are made scapegoats. In fact, most of the perpetrators of such acts go scot-free, by taking advantage of the legal loopholes and by manipulating evidence. The assumption is that markets can do no wrong and those who work within the system are safe from the Damocles' sword of corruption, although it is well known that market system works on greed and avarice, progenitors of corruption. It is those, in the fringe of the market system, but essential to the working of the market system, who come under the limited net of corruption. Even then the actions are more symbolic in nature, designed to assuage the temporary public outcry.

In any discussion on bureaucracy, politics must figure, because of the integrated relation between the two. In a democracy, bureaucracy is an integral part of the political system and has to prima facie accept a secondary role. Only in a dictatorship, can the bureaucracy have full sway, as we have seen in neighbouring Pakistan, where the military bureaucracy held on to power for nearly half a century. Corruption, which was the main plank on which the army came to power, was systemised under the new dispensation. In fact the talk of corruption ceased and the extent of corruption was known only after the change of a particular regime. The crescendo over corruption in most of the newly independent counties, have proved counter productive and has only provided ammunition to the vested interests to discredit the democratic system and extend their sway. The huge funding of the American elections, by persons or bodies unknown to the electorate, is a clear indicator of the various lobbies at play in election process. Obviously these lobbies will expect their quid pro quo in return. There are of course no lobbies of the marginalised section, which constitute the bulk of the population in any country. In India, fortunately, the lobby system has not yet, fully developed. However, this has resulted in some of the politicians taking to questionable methods to finance their elections and get into corrupt practices. The alternative is to have powerful lobbies of vested interests, which will control the democratic process. This will mean mockery of democracy in the Indian context with virtual disenfranchisement of the majority of the population, who will fail to organise themselves into powerful lobbies.

While wondering at the rapid economic progress of China in a short span of couple of decades and lamenting at our lack of economic foresight in opening our economy to the international economic forces, we should take a closer look at the Chinese polity vis-à-vis the Indian polity. It does not lie merely in the difference between the political systems adopted by the two countries, but in something more fundamental in the difference of psyche in both the countries. In India, politics is considered a necessary evil and politicians are talked about disparagingly, except the pre-independence ones, little realising the difference between agitational politics and governance. It is also naively assumed that if economic forces are allowed a free play and economists not politicians are at the helm of affairs, we will be able to emulate China. This country alone can be compared to India, because of its size and population. While in India, politics is disparaged, in China politics takes precedence over everything. An authority on China writes 'The development of the political sphere in the Chinese world and its pre-eminence over all the other (military, religious, economic) is one of its most characteristic marks'.[1] Whereas in India a myth was created during the long foreign rule that public ability did not exist in India. 'Thus grew the legend that public ability did not and never had existed in India, that proficiency in commerce and the law were the summit of modern Indian achievement.'[2] Then again 'Within the Company's territories personal relations, outside the sphere of commerce, tended more and more to be that of master and servant, the governor and the governed. So developed that contempt for things and persons Indian which was already prevalent in Calcutta in the time of Lord Hastings, and which produced the shallow half-truths of Mill and Macaulay and the downright contempt of lesser men.'[3] A very good recipe of keeping India under perpetual foreign domination! The subtle propaganda being Indians are good at everything, except governing themselves. After our independence this subtle propaganda has become a crescendo sometimes with media and the so-called intelligentsia making a major issue out of it.

The fact that all the elected governments since independence have remained pro-poor in varying degrees is certainly a major achievement of the Indian democracy. Of course, the intent has not always translated into desired results. This has invited ridicule and charges of corruption. In a feudalistic cum capitalistic set up, there are certainly major obstacles in implementing socialistic policies with the tools of the system. Bureaucracy alone cannot implement the policies in isolation and has to depend on the available socio-economic infrastructure, which is far from egalitarian. With new economic opportunities being made available through various government schemes for poverty alleviation, the existing powerful elements have benefited more than those, for whom the same were conceived. Market economy favours those who are already economically empowered and not those who are disentitled. Contractors and middlemen, who are essential for the implementation of the scheme, are from the economically dominant section and cannot be expected to be ideologically oriented towards egalitarianism.

These are not simplistic problems, which can be simply put down as conflict between politics and economics, as one being better than the other. General panacea is that politicians should not interfere in economic matters. Economic forces are not like the laws of gravity and are products of the existing socio-economic conditions. Politicians have a mandate from the electorate to improve these conditions and have to devise schemes to improve the economic conditions of the majority of the population. The existing socio-economic structure (popularly called vested interests), will naturally like to derail these and turn the same to their advantage. The problem is not simply political or bureaucratic corruption, but a clash of existing socio-economic forces with the forces of change.

While on the subject of political corruption, bureaucracy has also come up for criticism. According to some, this is the single most malaise, besetting the Indian bureaucracy. There can be no justification of bureaucratic corruption, as they do not have a constituency to nurse. But the problem of official corruption can best be addressed by systemic method, rather than penal methods and knee-jerk reactions. Over the years, financial system has presented several loopholes, which need to be plugged. Profligacy in government spending has sent wrong signals to the lower-level government staff. The high lifestyle of private sector executives has encouraged the tendency to keep up with the Joneses, which in turn has encouraged corruption. Closely functioning with the political system, bureaucracy has been a part of the real politic.

In most cases of political corruption, bureaucracy has to be privy to the same. Political executives have to function through the bureaucracy in our system. An officialdom, which goes by the rule book, will hardly serve the purpose. It is necessary to have a proactive set of officials, who are in the same wavelength as their political masters. In that way spoils system is very much in evidence in the Indian bureaucracy. Permanent bureaucracy of the British pattern hardly exists in India. While there is permanency of service, there is no permanency of tenure in India. In fact tenures in higher administrative posts are highly fluctuating and too short for anybody to be really effective. Of course, there are core groups of officials, close to the power centre, who enjoy a longer tenure and are essential to the system. Closeness to the power centre is the secret of bureaucratic longevity. However, rest of the higher bureaucracy, being footloose, can hardly settle down to their job, creating an atmosphere of uncertainty for themselves, as well as the general public. A footloose bureaucracy can hardly be an effective bureaucracy.

In the initial stage, immediately after independence, bureaucracy was regarded as a counter to politics, in that they were considered to be custodian and interpreter of rules. This would have put both in a confrontational path. However, the basic role of bureaucracy is to ensure rule of law. After an uneasy coexistence for a few years, there developed a close relation between the two. This marriage of convenience has to a great extent obliterated the line dividing the role of each other. The concept of independence of bureaucracy, without any safeguard for its independent functioning, is basically a myth. In view of this, it becomes an adjunct to the political system. However, in a democratic system, there has to be a distinction between a professional bureaucracy and a system of courtiers of yesteryears. Some amount of safeguard is necessary in the functioning of bureaucracy to ensure that it does not degenerate into courtier system. Since, we have a long history of courtier system, we have to ensure that the thin line between the two is not crossed.

Although the job of a government official is secure with constitutional provisions, backed by a strong judicial system, there is no safeguard in functioning, due to a lack of any tenure system. Bureaucracy generally functions in a climate of uncertainty, as there is no systemic support and individual whims and caprices matter more. Some people occasionally come up with the suggestion that the security of service, is the main reason for official inefficiency and a system of hire and fire by the boss is the key to efficiency. These people are naive enough to equate public service with working under an individual for his personal interest. In any case, a dominant section in the bureaucracy may not be completely averse to this idea, as it will give them enormous power over their colleagues and subordinates. However, if this is ever done, the uncertainty factor in government service will be paramount and the thin line dividing a professional bureaucracy from a courtier system will disappear. We have to decide, whether we want a system of professional bureaucracy or a group of courtiers, who may be talented, but working at the behest of their masters.

Bureaucracy has become politically savvy and has accepted a secondary role for itself. This has to a great extent done away with the system of checks and balances, so important in the functioning of a democratic government.

In fact the system of checks and balances, drawing ridicule as red tapism, has taken a back seat in the functioning of the government. This leaves various loopholes in the system, leading to the leakage of public funds. One of the main roles of the bureaucracy is to advice the political executive in a professional manner about policy formulation and its implementation. The former has to some extent been outsourced to various bodies (both Indian and foreign) outside the government. This trend is on the increase. The basic difficulty in this system is the lack of accountability of bodies outside the government involved in advising the government. When results have not been forthcoming as expected, bureaucracy has been under criticism and accused of lack of professionalism. This puts it in a defensive mode and consequently, there has been a tendency to salvage the situation by calling for advice from agencies outside the government system.

In the early stages, in the fifties, there was a modest beginning with foreign experts advising us on how to run our Panchayat Raj bodies.[4] The advice was hardly of any use and we had to go slow in our local self-government experiment for nearly two decades, i.e., seventies and eighties. In the sixties, we solved the major problem of food deficiency through the Green Revolution on our own, without any foreign aid or advice. In spite of this achievement, in the seventies we invited World Bank to aid and advice us in a big way for agricultural and rural development. This led to induction of foreign experts, not only for advice in technical matters, but also in administrative matters. Since then, there has been no looking back on foreign aid and advice. Consultancy bodies, both foreign and Indians have been advising the government in a major way. British Aid, rechristened as DFID (Department of International Development of the Government of United Kingdom), has played a major part in restructuring public sector in Orissa through their consultants. The Government of West Bengal is in the process of restructuring its public sector units with a grant of Rs. 184 crores from DFID. They are also playing a major part in the field of education and health administration in the States of Andhra Pradesh, Madhya Pradesh, Orissa and West Bengal. After having taken all the pains to get rid of the British administration, we have invited them back in a short span of a few years to handle our administration. Ironic indeed!

Dependence on advisers and experts of different hues has led to the marginalisation of the bureaucratic system. At the same time the bureaucracy is held responsible, when desired results are not achieved. Advisers bear no responsibility for the advice rendered by them, when things go wrong. The practice of frequently seeking advice on policy matters outside the government system has led to the loss of confidence in bureaucracy. Concept of government has also undergone a radical change in the process. According to Article 166 (3) of the Constitution of India, work of the government, is to be executed through rules of business. Functionaries, accordingly have to be Ministers with original powers and officials with delegated powers. Ministers come through the electoral process, whereas officials are selected by the Service Commission. The intention of the founders of the Constitution was to avoid the 'spoils system' in public service and have an independent civil service. Induction of outsiders in the government system was obviously not intended.

Choice of advisers, whether working individually or through committees, is the personal prerogative of the political executive and the legislature or the service commissions have no say in the matter. The principal advisers are appointed through personal selection and do not come through the usual bureaucratic process. In that way 'spoils system', is already in operation at the higher level of bureaucracy. This shows that the government machinery is more person-oriented than system oriented.

Bureaucracy as a system of governance has hardly developed in the Indian polity, although there are individuals of high calibre in the system. It is to be seen, whether we will have more of personalised system of governance, or greater faith will be imposed on the system. In case the present pattern of generalised bureaucracy, inherited from colonial days, does not evince much confidence, it may be better to go in for a different pattern, instead of attempting ad hoc solutions. However, politicians being generalists themselves, prefer to interact with the generalist bureaucracy. It is not that technical bureaucracy does not exist in the government system. There is no dearth of highly qualified specialists, in almost all the disciplines in the government system and there is hardly any need for outside advice. Obviously, there is loss of faith in the system, for which advisers from outside, have become the rule, rather than the exception. This creates a system of cronyism, which permeates the entire bureaucracy. In the prevailing situation, ship of the bureaucracy is certainly in uncharted waters.

-Kalyan Ray

Endnotes

1. Jacques Gernet, *A History of Chinese Civilization*, Second Edition (1996), translated by JR Foster and Charles Hartman, Cambridge University Press, p.28
2. Vincent A Smith, edited by Percival Spear, *The Oxford History of India*, Fourth Edition (1995), Oxford University Press, p.532.
3. Ibid, p. 533.
4. At the request of the Government of India, the United Nations Technical Assistance Administration appointed a Mission in 1961 for assessing the results so far achieved by the Community Development Programme. When the Mission undertook its study, the recommendations of the Balwaantrai Mehta Committee were in the process of implementation. The report of the Mission was in variance with the Mehta Committee report and was instrumental in shelving it. This resulted in slowing down Panchayat Raj movement for about twenty years.

Chapter- I

Introduction

Any discussion on bureaucracy generally raises extremes of passion, perhaps next only to politics, a pet hate subject for coffee table discussions. A general view is that if politics and bureaucracy can be eliminated, world will be a better place to live in. However, both of these are facts of life and cannot simply be wished away. As we cannot have democracy without politicians, it is not possible to have an orderly civilized society without a professional bureaucracy. The strong passion is due to the fact that bureaucracy touches everyone's life and one cannot simply do without it, whether one is a billionaire or a man in the street. During pre-independence period, bureaucracy did not attract much criticism, due to the fact that it was an agent of foreign rule and we had to accept whatever services were offered, without questioning the same. With the advent of independence, expectations from the government became high and there was a mismatch between expectations and results. This failure of expectations led to criticism of bureaucracy. At the same time the socio-economic complexities of the present day life have led to more of government in our life.

The adage 'the best form of government is one, which governs the least', does not hold good today, when more and more laws and rules are coming up to govern our daily life. However, there is a kernel of truth in the statement, that a society, which can manage its affairs better with least interference from the government and with less of rules and regulations, is certainly more desirable. The changing society of the modern day and fast emerging ideas on the need of more and more legislations, do not assure us of a situation in the near future and we will have to live with more and more laws to regulate ourselves. Laws and rules are to be administered and hence the need for bureaucracy. This will obviously lead to increase in bureaucracy, both administrative and quasi-judicial and its downsizing will hardly be possible.

Although one may not like bureaucracy, there seems to be no getting away from it and more we talk of having less of it, more we have of it. This is one of the paradoxes of modern day life. The attempt to have a free market economy by abolishing the Licence-Control Raj of the socialist days, should have led to a reduction in bureaucracy. But this has not happened. On the other hand, there has been sizeable increase in bureaucracy, by creation of a plethora of regulatory bodies at public expense. Free market economy cannot obviously do without government regulations. This has led to the creation of parallel bureaucratic organisations in all departments of government, with no reduction of staff and officials in the government departments. In fact, government cannot absolve itself of its sovereign power by delegating it to some other body. The government (executive wing) is answerable to the legislature for any act of omission or commission of any of the organisations, which are its creations. This trend of transferring powers of government to different statutory bodies, has led to government ministries being reduced to post offices. Development of a parallel bureaucracy with quasi-judicial powers, which is not answerable to the concerned minister, who is responsible to the legislature, is a development, which cannot be neglected by any serious student of Indian polity. Over the years, a quasi-judicial bureaucracy has come into existence in the form of various commissions, tribunals and regulatory bodies. These bodies occupy middle strata, between political executive and judiciary and enjoy complete independence from the political executive. These developments represent the trend to break free from the politico-bureaucratic system.

After independence, there was considerable expansion of bureaucracy, as the state took upon itself, the task of direct administration. Previously, lot of government work was handled indirectly through agents like Zamindars, who were entrusted with land revenue collection. Since taxation constitutes the sovereign power of government, after independence, immediate steps were taken to abolish the farming system of land revenue. There was also a system of village police or Chowkidars, in which a person was hereditarily appointed to the post, in lieu of a small land grant. This was a system in existence long before the British administration. This was also abolished. With the abolition of all sorts of intermediaries and assumption of direct responsibility by the government, there was need of a large number of government officials. In the initial stages, there were problems, because of the feudal system in existence in the ex-Zamindary areas and the ex-Princely states. It was difficult for lower level government officials to find acceptance and exercise the powers of the state over people long used to the feudal system. Breaking up of a feudal system, which has come down over generations, is hardly possible through legislation.

Lower level field staff, which constitutes the cutting edge of the bureaucracy, had a much lower level of acceptance and prestige than the erstwhile intermediaries, who were also the local gentry. Effectiveness of any administrative system depends on the level of acceptance and prestige it receives from the local populace. People long used to be administered by their social superiors, found it difficult to accept the authority of persons, whom they did not consider their social equals. I recollect the conversation I had with a respected leader of the Communist movement, who came from a rich landlord family of Bengal. He was pragmatic enough to tell me that his father, who belonged to the old school, gave up his landed interest and business, not for any ideological reasons, but simply due to the fact that he was unwilling to have dealings with revenue inspectors and supply inspectors, who were well below him in the social ladder. This also explains the fact, why many of the educated middle class voters are unwilling to go to the polling stations to cast their vote, due to their reluctance to interact with the lower order polling staff. The field staff with inadequate motivation and remuneration, having enormous power of the state at their disposal, hardly knows how to utilise the same and will tend to misutilise the same unless a proper system of checks and balances, is put in place.

The present system of supervision and audit is too inadequate to enforce proper accountability and discharge of duties. In fact, it is on the performance of the cutting edge bureaucracy (which has also been called the street level bureaucracy) that the success and failure of a government programme depends. The elitist concept of bureaucracy, which we have inherited from colonial days, has taken them for granted and has failed to address their problems. The cliche' that Indian Civil Service was the Steel Frame, which held up the administration in pre-independence days, has been the basis of most of the administrative thinking. We have to understand that any system is as strong or weak as the weakest link in the chain and not the strongest link. The government machinery is also too thinly spread to be really effective.

The remedy does not lie in having an all pervasive government machinery, but in developing a self administering system. The age old Panchayat system, which was based on social prestige of its constituents, has to be revived by democratising it and making it more broad based.

Governance is an art, of which administration constitutes a part. The art of governance in a democracy involves both the parties - people and government officials. Basically in a democracy, the people should govern themselves; government machinery should only be a catalytic agent. The long period of foreign rule, created rulers and subjects, in which one rules and the other is a subject. British officers had no doubts that they were the rulers, ruling over a subject nation. This is borne out by memoirs published with nostalgic titles, such as '*The Men Who Ruled India*'[1]. They were for the services of the Empire, continuance of which was their foremost goal. There is a gulf which separates administration and ruling. While, the British were ruling India, the administration of their own country, was far from satisfactory. To cite an example, their experimentations in the nineteenth century with poverty alleviation schemes, such as 'Poor Laws', were so much bogged down by corruption and maladministration, that these had to be abolished by Act of Parliament, creating immense distress for the poor. Distress was relieved by their policy of acquiring colonies of immigration like Australia[2]. Even their administration of socialistic policies, after the Second World War, when they were free of their colonial burden, was hardly successful and had to be completely modified or given up. We certainly do not have the luxury to abolish our poverty alleviation schemes, in the name of market economy, without inviting serious social unrest.

With increase in economic disparity and no visible sign of poverty reduction, except in some sample survey statistics, a democratically elected government will have to go in for more and more poverty alleviation schemes. This will call for greater role for professional bureaucracy, in the absence of any viable alternative. Basically, we have two tiers of bureaucracy, appointed by the Central Government and the state governments. The poverty alleviation schemes are mostly funded by the Centre and executed by the states. This dichotomy of funding agency and executing agency creates its own problems, as the funds are time bound and have to pass through a long channel of checks and balances. The state government takes up execution of work through its own agencies, manned by its own employees. This to a great extent is responsible for lack of local involvement. To create greater local involvement, it is necessary that local elected bodies are made responsible for execution of projects, which require grassroot involvement.

There is necessity of developing a third tier of bureaucracy, responsible to the local bodies, as in the case of urban local bodies. Of course, there will be necessity to put in adequate checks and balances in place, to ensure proper functioning of the schemes. It is also necessary to develop institutions like beneficiary groups to ensure that their interests are taken care of. It is necessary that the mechanism of self government is developed at the local level, as envisaged in the Constitution. Good governance from the Centre or state cannot be a substitute for self governance at the local level. It will not be adequate to simply transfer power to the local bodies. A system of responsibilities has to be built into it. As was envisaged earlier, local bodies in non urban areas should have power of taxation within their jurisdiction, with the provision that they should contribute to the development process. Financial discipline can be introduced in the local bodies only by enabling them to raise their own resources, instead of depending on distant funds.

In comparatively developed areas, local bodies do generate some resources, but hardly spend the same on any poverty alleviation programme, as these are thought to be the responsibility of Centre or state. Taking care of indigent people should be made the statutory responsibility of local panchayats and if necessary, funds should be provided for the same. A third tier of bureaucracy at the local level, responsible to the local bodies, is essential for taking administration to the grassroot level. Instead of academic excellence, experience in social service, should be the criterion for selection to these posts.

We have inherited a centralised system of administration from pre 1947 times, where the system rotated round a single authority in the centre, province or the district. Administration through such remote control mechanism may be successful in normal times, but it has serious limitations in difficult times. This was clearly demonstrated during the last decade of British rule in India. The failure to tackle the Bengal famine of 1943, when millions of people perished, shows the complete failure of the administrative machinery to provide the minimum sustenance to the people to survive. Famines have been more frequent during the British rule than during the earlier period in the Indian history.[3] Similarly, there was complete failure of administration to protect the lives of the people, during the riots of 1946 and 1947.

Remote control administration from the Central or provincial headquarters completely failed in such a situation. Test of an administrative system lies in successfully confronting an emergency situation and in providing relief to the people. In both these counts, pre-independence administration was a failure, in spite of numerous memoirs by the erstwhile rulers, eulogising their own roles. *Mai-Baap* governance is not the way to good administration, as *Mai-Baaps* cannot be present everywhere. Solution for good governance and administration lies in having robust institutions for self governance at the local level. In this, British colonial policy was in contrast to Roman colonial policy, which developed local self governing institutions in provinces, which came under the Roman rule.

During the long period of foreign rule, particularly British rule, self governing institutions at the local level withered away. Denied the opportunity of self governance, public ability withered at the local level. Although, at the national or provincial levels, seats of governments, where they could see the governments in action, public spirited individuals kept a watch on governmental proceedings. They were equal to or even better than the so-called rulers, when given the opportunity. However, the fact remains that, one had to come to the national or provincial headquarters to prove his worth. Persons of ability gravitated to these places. Drained of talents and opportunity, local leadership had no opportunity to develop. A paternalistic administration, where people are treated as passive objects, lulls them into somnambulism. Had local self-governing bodies been in place with adequate powers, things might have been different in the forties and a great deal of tragedy could have been avoided. Absence of properly empowered local bodies left the provincial government completely high and dry to deal with such situations. In matters of crisis, local leadership with administrative ability will be more effective than distant government, in spite of having the best of intentions.

West Bengal experienced a civil war like situation in the late seventies, with the Naxalite movement taking a firm root in the state. The movement had its ideological base in its support from a large number of intellectuals, who dissatisfied with the existing system, openly advocated a war against the state. The serious law and order aspects of the problem could be controlled by the police, with full government support, by waging a war of sorts against the extremist elements. Naxalite movement was not a workers' movement, nor was there large-scale peasant uprising. The movement was spearheaded by educated youth, who were disenchanted by the existing socio-economic order, for which they held the state responsible and advocated its overthrow. These youths targeted the lower level government functionaries and wanted to spread their message through violence. Police identified their target effectively and replied in kind. This put a stop to extremist adventurism. Had it been a full scale peasant uprising, it might not have been possible to stop it by police action.

These types of movements generally go underground when state action is intensified and resurfaces when normalcy is restored. On record, the movement with its accompanying violence did not resurface for quite sometime. But, there seems to be simmering discontent and the problem was merely swept under the carpet. The state was not free from sporadic violence and group clashes during the intervening period. It has resurfaced since the eighties with a vengeance. This time, it does not seem to be the typical middle class movement orchestrated by frustrated educated youth and the problem seems deeper and is yet to be fathomed. However, there seems to be a major problem of alienation, with a large section of the society.

West Bengal offers a classic case of use/misuse of the Panchayati system. It was one of the first states to activate the panchayati machinery since 1977, with lot of powers of the state government being delegated to these local self governing bodies. Empowerment of local bodies had paid dividends in development of the rural economy through increased agricultural productivity and all-round economic development. Land reforms laws, relating to more equitable land holdings could be effectively implemented under the supervision of Panchayati bodies.

Success of the programme of distribution of surplus land (land held in excess by big landholders and resumed by the government according to the statute) amongst the landless peasants, took care of their grievance and they used the newly acquired asset to improve their economic wellbeing, instead of falling prey to any extremist ideology. Agricultural productivity increased significantly. There was also no case of starvation death, which embarrassed many other state governments from time to time. It is not always possible for the state machinery to reach out to all the indigent people in distant corners of the state, unless it has adequate support system, which can only be provided by empowered and elected local bodies, not by a bureaucracy controlled from the state headquarters. With local self-government being activated, governance process was set in motion at the village level and the local grievances could be better addressed. For a considerable period, West Bengal was considered a model state for democratic decentralization and rural development.

The picture was not as rosy, as was pictured outside rural Bengal, through a favourable publicity, at least for a decade and half, although the good wok done in rural areas in the early stages cannot be denied. However, democracy can function, only when a strong opposition is there. Intolerance of opposition is not congenial for the functioning of any democratic institution. Opposition to the ruling party was wiped out through patronage or muscle, aided and abetted by state power. The functionaries at the panchayat level had become party cadres of the ruling party at the state level and had eliminated all opposition at the village level. These functionaries enjoyed absolute power and became a law unto themselves, under the protection and patronage of the government machinery. Panchayats became the den of vested interests. By owing allegiance to the party in power in the state government, the elected panchayat leaders gained full control over the local government officials, particularly Police and Land & Land Revenue departments. This method cut across the usual channels of control in the government system. This was in fact a re-run of the Soviet system. Panchayat functionaries, once elected, became a part of the party machinery of the ruling party in the state government. They became party appartchiks[5] and bureaucratized the system, instead of functioning as elected representatives.

Success of the functioning of a democratic society depends on the successful working of the base level democracy. This was certainly realised by the Constitution makers and was enshrined in Article 40 of the Directive Principles of State Policy of this momentous document. However, after some initial attempt in this direction, the process was discontinued and the panchayat institutions had become moribund. Enactment of 73rd Amendment Act of Constitution of India in 1992 gave a new lease of life to these institutions. Part IX, Article 243 of the Constitution makes it mandatory for the state governments to hold regular elections for the panchayats and make arrangements for their finances. The Amendment aims at making these bodies, the third tier of democracy. However, this experiment is yet to give any substantial result.

Panchayat bodies to be effective must have necessary infrastructure in the shape of supporting staff. This will require another tier of bureaucracy, besides those at the centre and state levels. Since the jobs at this level are basic in nature, supervisory staff should be kept at a minimum. Incentive should be provided by giving better career opportunities to central or state government officials of all categories, who are willing to work at the panchayat or village level. This will, of course, require a new work culture than what we have been accustomed to at present.

We inherited the secretariat pattern of public service from the erstwhile regime and have continued with it ever since. Over the years, secretariat has grown manifold in size, quite disproportionate to the growth of staff at the execution level (also known as cutting edge staff). There has been, of course, considerable expansion of police force, along with their powers. But, administrative staff, dealing directly with the people, has not increased proportionately. This clearly goes to show that the administrative system is an end in itself, rather than a means to an end. The administrative pyramid is clearly lopsided with preponderance of higher policy-making and supervisory bureaucracy. Undue importance of the secretariat pattern of administration effectively dilutes responsibility. It is like having a huge army with majority of the officers and soldiers engaged in staff duty, rather than operational duty. Secretariat pattern of administation is in evidence everywhere in the administrative system. From the gigantic secretariats at the Central and state levels, to the palatial offices of the various heads of departments, housing their enormous staff, is a spectacle indeed of the majesty of the government. Even those down the line, have their own secretariats. At the district level, Collectorate is a huge secretariat, which has grown over the years. Management of such a huge office makes the Collector desk bound at the cost of his executive duties. All the officials of various departments at different levels have their own offices, which are miniature secretariats. Office management takes up lot of time of executive officials at the cost of their executive duties.

The basic concept in today's administration is that no official can discharge his duties effectively without adequate supporting staff at the office level. Bigger the office, greater is the importance of the official. The result has been the growth of a huge army of officials for support duty, without any direct responsibility. Large number of government employees are engaged in unproductive work and could be better utilised in executive functions. This will also solve the perennial problem of shortage of staff at the cutting edge level and improve the delivery system of government machinery, without additional cost to the state exchequer. An efficient administrative system should have more people at the execution level, rather than at the staff level. This will also go a long way in improving the morale of a large number of government employees, who have hardly any job satisfaction under the present dispensation.

Village level worker is the basic developmental functionary, with a number of villages under his charge. He deals directly with the people and can be considered to be the cutting edge staff for various programmes of both Central and state governments. Although, he is an employee of the state government, he is charged with efficient execution of number of schemes, formulated by various departments of Government of India, Central Planning Commission, various International Agencies like World Bank and others, besides the work of his employer, the state government. A formidable list of masters indeed, for a low paid government employee. The success or failure of schemes formulated at huge expense by a battery of high level experts and officials depends on this single individual at the execution level. Of course, there are number of supervisory officers to oversee his work, but hardly anybody to assist him. He also has a new set of masters, in the form of various NGOs from the national or state capitals, who send their agents to question him and evaluate his work. Hopes and aspirations of the country revolve round the efficient and sincerity of this individual at the bottom of the administrative ladder. A real paradox indeed, where the huge administrative pyramid rests on a thin edge!

Need for a huge array of supporting staff is a throwback on colonialism and feudalism, which mindset, we have been unable to get rid of. In fact this has been further fine tuned, with greater opportunity in present times. Bureaucracy in fact mirrors the society, more than anything else. Culture of courtiers or innumerable advisors or hangers-on, so necessary for Rajas and Maharajas or their potentates for discharge of their duties, is as much a necessity today, as it was earlier. With availability of Computers and other tools of office management, there is scope for rationalisation of office staff (particularly a large number of helpers) and proportionate increase of executive staff. In fact, computerization has created another set of staff. The existing staffing pattern mostly remains undisturbed, as there is need for manual back up, due to frequent problems with the computer systems. Computers after all are not infallible and are frequently affected by viruses. Some of the more sophisticated machines, acquired by government offices, have a tendency to break down, under tropical climatic conditions. These sensitive gadgets have been designed under different climatic conditions, which cannot always be replicated. This often creates problems, as the old system of paper work, has been discontinued.

Training of higher officials in our time did not include basic knowledge of an important tool of office administration like typing. This makes an officer dependant on his typist or stenographer. Efficiency of the officer depends to a great extent on his stenographer. Similarly, knowledge of office management like filing of documents, maintenance of records, docketing of files, maintenance of registers are thought to be too plebian to be included in the curriculum of the higher officials in the training academies. This is the domain of the ministerial staff and is taught in their training schools. Without basic knowledge of the tools of office administration, the officer is fully dependant on his ministerial staff. This leads to ridiculous situations some times, when important official work is held up due to the non-availability of a particular file, because of the absence of the concerned clerk, who is the custodian of the file. The importance of the ministerial staff lies in the fact that they are the custodians of the files and documents, without which government work cannot move. Division of labour is extremely rigid in government offices and is akin to the caste system. This rigid segregation of work creates a culture of dependency, which is on the increase over the years.

In the early years of our service career, ostentation was looked down upon and a comparatively simple lifestyle was maintained. There were hardly any staff cars and the higher officials were coming in their own small cars, by driving themselves. Even the ministers of the government used to come in their private cars, purchased through government loans. This was not merely the case in the backwaters of administration. Even in colonial Britain of the fifties, Winston Churchill, then the Leader of the Opposition had to hire a cab on his own to reach the House of Commons for delivering his famous speech on Cold War, which ushered in an era of diplomatic offensive. Today with a battery of chauffer driven government cars in evidence everywhere, such a situation looks to be prehistoric.

With ostentation increasing all-round, government functionaries can hardly be expected to lead an outdated lifestyle. In earlier times, the private sector executives also maintained a fairly unostentatious standard of living. It was thought to be indecent to make a show of one's wealth or position. The social values have undergone a sea change over a single generation and today ostentation is the in thing and according to the predominant economic belief, powers our development. More important a person is in the official hierarchy, greater is his dependence on the supporting staff. The importance of a government functionary depends on the number of staff directly serving him. Dependency on so many disparate functionaries has the effect of bogging down the efficiency of a higher functionary to the level of lowest common denominator. The weakest link in the chain will pull down an efficient individual. An organisation is as weak or strong as the weakest individual in the chain. In this system, punctuality of the officials depends on the punctuality of the drivers.

An elitist bureaucracy, hemmed in by a circle of helpers, further isolates it. One has to penetrate several layers of supporting officials to approach the top. This is of course as much applicable to political executives, as to the bureaucracy. A large army of personal staff, maintained at public cost leads to great deal of direct and indirect influence on government administration on the part of these functionaries. In fact this pattern of administration, where the personal staff of both political and bureaucratic executive, have grown from strength to strength, can hardly be ignored by a serious observer of Indian public administration. This method cuts across the normal organisational pattern and makes the administrative machinery individual oriented, rather than system oriented. It must be mentioned, that this development is not confined to government organisations alone, both public and private sector top executives have a huge army of personal staff constituted into Chairman's and Managing Director's Secretariat.

Studies of any formal organisation have been generally confined to analysing the working of line and staff agencies. This has also been the case with classic works on public administration, where the organisation is divided into line and staff functionaries. Line agency consists of chain of executive staff for administration of government programmes. Staff agency consists of officials organised in the Secretariat pattern, in a hierarchical pattern, working under Rules of Business of Government. This set of rules formalises the working of the Government Secretariat and is essential for the impartial functioning of the government machinery. Personal Secretariats of higher functionaries, which are in fact their think tanks and decision making tools, have substituted the working of the formal Secretariat. These establishments do not function under Rules of Business for government departments and are free to chart out their own course of action.

This parallel Secretariat, which does not come under either line or staff agency, has made the official Secretariat redundant to a great extent. Important decisions emanate from the top and the official secretariat is given the task of processing and conveying the same, to give it a stamp of government decision. Result has been to make the bureaucracy person oriented, rather than system oriented. Impartial administrative machinery is essential in a democratic polity. Strength of any organisation depends on its institutional viability. Persons come and go, but the institution must survive beyond them. Institution building is of greater importance than any immediate gains.

Attempts to cut through the Red Tape should not lead to side stepping due procedures. Judicial system cannot think of doing away with the time tested court procedures in the name of instant justice. Had this been attempted, there would have been grave miscarriage of justice and erosion of judicial credibility. An institution takes years to develop and is not the handiwork of a single individual or group. Bureaucratic institutions are under challenge today. This may be partly because we have inherited most of these institutions from colonial times. But this is also equally applicable to the educational and judicial systems. Obviously, there is a crisis of public expectations from the bureaucratic system, which is linked to the political system. To meet such a situation, ad hoc solutions like personalised bureaucracy, revolving round a few individuals in authority, is not the solution. This will only create an authoritarian bureaucracy, which will not be in consonance with our democratic constitution. Any democratic institution has to be procedure oriented, rather than person oriented. This is fundamental to the rule of law. The procedure may be slow, as judicious functioning cannot be done in a hurry. Decisions taken in a hurry are generally not the best decisions, as all the pros and cons are not considered. Unless; we are able to evolve a better system, existing system of checks and balances, should not be tampered with. Checks and balances were designed to ensure impartiality, objectivity and integrity, which seem to be in short supply these days. In fact, doing away with time tested procedural checks, in pursuit of quick results, has created the monster of corruption. Bureaucracy is thus caught between the Scylla and Charybdis of red tapism and corruption.

Endnotes

1. Philip Woodruff, *The Men Who Ruled India, Vol. I, The Founders; Vol. II, The Guardians (1954)*, Jonathan Cape, London.
2. Kalyan Ray, *Globalization or Colonisation?* (2004), Deep & Deep Publications Pvt. Ltd., Delhi.
3. Famine Inquiry Commission (1945) of Government of India, put the death toll at 1.5 million. But this was an under estimation, as years later in 1979, WR Aykroyd, who was a member of the Famine Inquiry Commission and was primarily responsible for the estimates, conceded that the figures were an under-estimation. Aykroyd said "I now think it (the death toll) was an under-estimate, especially in that it took little account of roadside deaths". By all reliable accounts, the death toll related to starvation and

consequences thereof was in the region of about 5 million. This was the epilogue of the so called 'white man's burden' in giving an efficient administration to the natives.

4. Open letters of Romesh C Dutt to Lord Curzon, Viceroy of India in 1900 and Speeches delivered by him between 1900-1902.

   Reprinted as 'Open Letters to Lord Curzon' (1986) by Gian Publishing House, Delhi.

5. Appartchik (functionary) is a Russian colloquial term for a full-time professional functionary of the Communist Party or government; i.e., an agent of the governmental or party 'appart' (apparatus).

Chapter- II

Licence Control Raj to Corporate Raj

Corruption and Governance seem to have been closely interlinked in public mind. This has created a great deal of disaffection towards government, which is dangerous for a democratic polity. When people talk of corruption, it is generally financial corruption. But this is only a visible aspect of corruption. Nepotism and favouritism are some of the main manifestations of corruption in the use of authority. Putting one's relations, friends and cohorts in important places has become an important feature of public service. Of course, most of the private sector companies have made this system institutionalized in recent times. It is the sons, daughters, close relations and friends, who are in positions of authority in the corporate sector units since the eighties. However, in the government machinery, such a system will be the very negation of the concept of public service.

Whenever there is a change of government, a set of advisors (mostly retired) as experts surfaces. They are mostly freelancers and owe their positions mostly to their proximity to the Prime Minister or any other important power centres. They function like a shadow cabinet and exercise more power than the regular cabinet. Secretaries or advisors to the Prime Minister or Chief Minister in a state are powerful posts indeed. In fact, they are the power behind the throne. Since these are not constitutional posts, accountability of these functionaries to the Parliament do not exist. They are personally accountable only to the Prime Minister/Minister. Since all the political parties have been following this practice, nobody raises any question. From this practice, it is a small step to a personalized and closed bureaucracy. Everybody's thinking must be in the same wavelength and must be in sync with the boss. Anybody with a different view will be the odd man out. This is virtually the end of an independent bureaucracy. In such a situation, any independent or objective view can hardly be offered. Without any effective system of checks and balances, use of absolute and arbitrary power is but one step. Power and its improper use is the main source of corruption. When we talk of power, it is the state power, which we have in mind. But the state machinery does not operate in isolation. Over the years, a system of power brokers has developed in the corridors of power, both in the centre and the states. They operate piggy back on the government machinery and have enormous clout.

Scandals of corruption seem to be an integral part of self-governance, whether at the centre, state or panchayat level. This gives credence to the oft repeated British adage that we are incapable of governing ourselves. Some vocal sections seem to be coming round to the view that we are not capable of governing ourselves. Well meaning people are throwing up their hands and are suggesting that government should withdraw from various legitimate spheres of activities and hand over the same to the private sector through outsourcing. This is due to a new found belief of the nineties (post socialism) in the efficacy of the market mechanism and that market can do no wrong. The belief in market god has received serious jolts time to time from various securities scams, Satyam scam, 2G scam, Radia tapes, amongst others.

The basic question arises that while Indians are good at almost all spheres of activities, how is it that we are falling short in the art of governance. This has been the situation right from the days of foreign rule. The answer probably lies in the long periods of foreign rule, which India has endured. During these long stretches, Indians were effectively excluded from governance. The foreign rulers had Indian employees through whom they carried out their day to day administration. Sometimes, they had Indians as advisors. But, the fact remains that they were basically employees and had limited role assigned by their masters. Foreign rulers governed according to their interests and according to their own values. System of values of rulers and ruled cannot be the same. Relation between ruler and ruled is one between master and servant. Good rule cannot be the same as self rule. A good foreign ruler can at best be patronizing or condescending. Long period of exclusion from governance has led to atrophy of the art of governance among the Indians. Governance is the supreme art, which takes ages and generations to develop. Mankind has been struggling, ever since their existence for developing a viable system of government, but without much success. An art, which has languished for centuries, cannot be revived immediately or within a span of few decades. In the meantime, peoples' patience is running out. This is the tragedy of countries, which have been under long foreign rule. In the euphoria of newly found independence, the responsibility of self-governance is forgotten.

Corruption - Pre-Independence

Corruption seems to be haunting the government from the beginning of self rule. Complaints of corruption against the governments formed in six states by the Congress Party under the 1935 Act, reached Mahatma Gandhi, the spiritual leader of the party. Gandhi, in his inimitable style reacted to the outburst in May, 1939, 'I would go to the length of giving the whole congress a decent burial, rather than put up with the corruption that is rampant'. (Quoted from South Asia Analysis Group, paper no. 219 by R Upadhyay, dated 30.03.2001). Of course, he could not have meant it very seriously. It was the anguished outpouring of a moralist, who dreamt of Ram Raj, once foreign rule was replaced by Indian rule. But like the proverbial Utopia, Ram Raj exists only in the realm of imagination and has not been in existence anywhere in recorded history. However, Gandhi took the matter seriously enough to punish the Congress ministers by asking them to resign from the government, wherever the party was in power. Probably, he wanted them to go for a period of soul searching in political wilderness. Resignation of Congress ministries was greeted by Jinnah as 'day of deliverance and thanksgiving, as a mark of relief that the Congress regime had at last ceased to function'. This paved the way for the Muslim League to come to power, with their agenda of direct action and partition of the country, which Gandhi had vehemently opposed. It is on record that he had said that partition of the country would take place over his dead body. But, ultimately he had to accept the situation in the wake of huge civil war in Punjab and Bengal. Absence of Congress Party, the only party with a pan-Indian outlook, from the government machinery in the states, allowed the Muslim League to carry out their policy of encouraging communal riots and ultimately partition. Withdrawing from the government by riding the moral high horse proved costly for the country in the long run. It was like handing over power to the enemy on a platter. In fact the prime agenda of the Congress Party of keeping the country united was lost. Had the Congress Party been in power, massive communal riots, which took place due to the absence or connivance of the government machinery, could have certainly been avoided or minimised.

Why have we been plagued by the smoke of scandals right from the inception of self rule, leading to the resignation of the Congress ministries in pre-Independent India? The successor Muslim League ministry did not consist of a bunch of angels either. Complaints of corruption were galore against many of these ministers. Muslim League ministry in Bengal was mired in corruption and mismanagement of food supply. There were serious allegations in the Press and different quarters that Ispahani Group of Companies, who was a major trading agent, had indulged in hoarding and diversion of large quantities of food-grains, meant for famine hit areas. No action was taken against this trading house, as their owners were close to the then Chief Minister of the State (designated as Prime Minister at that time), HS Suhrawardy and MA Jinnah, the main architect of Pakistan. Character of Suhrawardy has been aptly summed up by the British journalist Leonard Mosley, who knew him at close quarters in his book 'The Last Days of the British Raj' (p.26): "Mr. Suhrawardy was a party 'boss' of the type who believes that no politician needs ever be out of office once his strong-arm squads have gained control of the polling booths. He loved money and was reputed to have made a fortune during the war".

In fact Suhrawardy's tactics of remaining in office perpetually was more successfully followed by the Left Front government in West Bengal, once they came to power with Jyoti Basu as Chief Minister. Using local goons to capture polling booths was the favoured tactics of the CPI (M) in West Bengal. Remaining in power, they had also perfected the art of using the official machinery to their advantage. This is a new variant of one party rule in a democracy, in which all the paraphernalia of the system is maintained. In the earlier stages, the Election Commission had no separate machinery to oversee the election process and was dependent on the state governments for carrying out the election process. West

Bengal was the first state, where a particular political party gained complete control of the political system, by organizing the employees into unions sponsored by the party. This together with the tactics of organizing the party cadres right up to the village level through local teachers, police and the revenue officials made the party invincible in the election arena. The party did not flinch from employing strong arm tactics, wherever their supremacy was challenged. Well oiled party machinery at the panchayat/village level was built up by entrusting the party cadres and sympathisers with development work through the panchayats, which were under the control of the ruling party. Functionaries at that level were given a free hand and the government machinery played a secondary role. Departmental control over government funds was hardly in existence in the name of delegation of power to panchayat bodies. Nobody dared challenge the dictates of the party bosses at the local level and they became a law unto themselves. There were reports of diversion and misappropriation of government funds by the local functionaries. But any detailed audit by the central audit machinery was effectively blocked in the name of state autonomy.

In the earlier stages, individual cases of corruption were not much heard of, although, it was frequently reported in the local Press that the son of the Chief Minister (Jyoti Basu), who was close to some business houses, was being unduly favoured. However, the opposition never pursued the matter seriously, as they themselves were rumoured to be beneficiary of government largesse. Communist sensibilities did not prevent the Chief Minister from going on regular sojourns at government expense with his relatives and retinue. The other ministers, however, did not enjoy this privilege. In the opposite end of the political spectrum, the Prime Minister in the BJP government, Atal Behari Vajpayee religiously followed the practice of going on long holidays to exotic destinations with relations and retinue, to rejuvenate the poet in him.

Ostentation and Corruption

While we may grudge the holidays at public cost of some of our elected representatives, we do not have any problems with the lavish and brazen lifestyle of our Corporate Barons, when they gift their wives jet planes as their birthday presents. They throw lavish wedding and birthday parties, costing crores, for their offsprings. They compete with each other in building magnificent palaces in the best locations. These are events, which the Press laps up. It will be tantamount to blasphemy to criticize them, as they have the magic wand, which creates wealth. Mahatma Gandhi's advice to businessmen with nationalist outlook that they are trustees of public funds has been completely forgotten and is probably an outdated concept in the days of brash consumerism. It is conveniently forgotten that their wealth is built from country's limited natural resources, including scarce land in an over populated country. Over utilization of the same has created serious social tensions and environmental damage. Most of these industrial empires have been built up on generous loans from public sector banks. The NPA (Non performing assets) list of the public sector banks is a virtual Who is Who of big business, which are the major defaulters. There was a demand by the Left parties and the Banking Unions during the BJP rule, when Yashwant Sinha was the Finance Minister, to direct the public sector banks to publish a list of major defaulters, particularly since the banks were facing financial crunch during that period. However, this was effectively stone walled for fear of offending the mighty corporate houses. Had the list been published, depositors and general public would have known the exposure of their banks in big business and their failure to return huge amounts of depositors money advanced to them.

One of the indexes of corruption is indecent ostentatious living. Weddings and birthday parties have become multi-crore affairs. Today's nouveau riche want to flaunt their ill-gotten wealth in the most brazen way. Recently, I came across a news item in the tabloid press regarding the wedding bashes of the siblings of two small time Congress leaders at Jaunapur village near Delhi, costing 250 crores of rupees. It was reported that the bridegroom was gifted a five-seater helicopter by the bride's father Sukhbir Singh Jaunpuria, an ex-MLA and wore a garland of one thousand rupee notes. Bridegroom is the son of Kanwar Singh Tanwar, a Congress leader, who is a transport operator and was the richest man contesting the last Assembly polls in Delhi. The guests list consisted of the glitterati of Bollywood and important political leaders, including the Prime Minister, who is unlikely to have attended. It would have been difficult for a political Prime Minister to avoid this event, due to electoral necessities. This is not an isolated event. Only thing special about it is the gift of a helicopter. Such wedding bashes with free flowing money have become the order of the day and Press and the public hardly take notice of the same.

All this money could not have been earned in a fair way and if there is proper investigation by the income tax department and the enforcement agencies, the sources of these funds can be unearthed. But nobody wants to spoil a party, particularly since the state has taken a hands free approach in these matters. Unlike in earlier times, people are not shy to flaunt their ill-gotten wealth. Previously, people with ill-gotten wealth were afraid of public opinion, attached with social stigma and hesitated to display their wealth. Post-liberalization, people's attitudes have changed and no eyebrows are raised. In fact, there is competition in lavish spending. With a huge parallel economy, a large portion of unaccounted money finds its way to ostentatious expenditure. This huge expenditure, whether in black or white money, contributes to our ever increasing GDP. It will be a bold income tax officer, who will review these expenditures inviting the ire of our economic pundits. India's performance in managing the economy is being judged primarily by the GDP figures and any shortfall from the same will be viewed seriously by the Finance Ministry and above all by the *pink newspapers*. When growth depends on ostentatious expenditure and speculations in real estate and stock market, very little can be done to curb the flow of black money in the economy. It is in fact the presence of huge unaccounted money in the country, which is the main cause of corruption. The trail of all black money does not necessarily lead to Swiss banks. There is plenty of black money within the country, which is doing immense damages to the economy and the social fabric. Unless some attempt is made to ferret out this money, any effort to tackle corruption will be futile. Any meaningful endeavour to stem the rot should begin at its very roots.

In the urban areas, speculations in land prices have made people rich over night. Real estate has been an important sector fueling economic growth, but this is a sector largely controlled by land mafia. With growing urbanization, there is ever growing demand for land for residential purposes in urban conglomerates. State governments do not have any clear cut policy in this regard and the entire thing is left to realtors. Land records are mostly not reliable. Complicated tenancy laws have made change of land use from agricultural to residential difficult. Civil litigations regarding ownership of land are galore. Large tracts of government land are under encroachment. Huge areas of prime lands have been allotted to different institutions. Mechanical uses of forest laws in the name of environment protection have further complicated the matter. Even if one gets a small plot of land from a government agency, one cannot be sure whether one will get a proper title over it. In India, marketability of land is very difficult due to disputed and multiple ownership in most cases.

Corruption and Armed Forces

Due to historical reasons, large areas of prime government land are in occupation of defence department, in the shape of cantonments and other military facilities. Obviously, realtors have their eyes on these prime properties. Sharad Pawar, who is market savvy, wanted to free some of the defence land, when he was Defence Minister in the Narsimha Rao cabinet. He had also made a statement to that effect. However, he did not have too long a tenure and nothing much was heard about the matter. In recent years, number of top ranking defence officials, were found involved in improper use of lands. This was also highlighted in the media. Two recent scams in which senior army officers were involved are Sukhna land deal and Adarsh Housing Society allotments in Mumbai. In the Sukhna case in Darjeeling district of West Bengal, Lt Gen PK Rath, Commander of Army's 33 Corps stationed there was charged with issuing a no objection certificate for state government land (measuring 71 acres), adjacent to the military cantonment, to set up a branch of well known Mayo College of Ajmer, through franchisee Geetanjali Education Trust (of realtor Dalip Aggarwal). Ealier, during the period of Rath's predecessor, the same land was leased out by the state government to another private party to set up a resort to promote tea tourism. Army objected to setting up a resort on security grounds. Obviously, a number of realtors was interested in acquiring this land and state government was keen to lease out the land. In such a scenario, it is better to have an institution, providing educational facilities to the children of army personnel posted in the unit, than to have a tourist resort, which is basically playground of the rich and is unlikely to have any good influence on the troops. Rath had kept the army headquarters at Delhi informed and the Secretary to the Chief of Staff had full knowledge of the same. The mistake Rath seems to have made was in not keeping Lt Gen VK Singh, GOC Eastern Command at Kolkata informed. This probably led to a clash of egos. At the same time Rath's preference for a school in place of the resort must have annoyed the realtors, promoting the same. These people will not hesitate in going to the Press with their own version of the matter and raising muck, once their interest is affected. Real estate lobby is a powerful one and can influence the media. Media, which is always in the look out for a story, blew the matter out of proportion. In such cases, officials due to their service rules are not able to defend themselves in the Press and public and a one-sided propaganda campaign is launched through the media. Once this happens, the officials stand condemned in public perception, before any enquiry in the matter can be made. What is, however most disturbing, is the turf war within the higher echelons of the armed forces. Findings of the Court of Inquiry were leaked to the Press, before any decision could be taken by the higher authority, thus pre-judging the issue. The officials were caught up in the cross-fire between the then Chief of Army Staff (Gen Deepak Kapoor) and the General Officer Commanding, Eastern Command (Lt Gen VK Singh, who was to succeed Kapoor). If a General level officer cannot be trusted with issuing a 'no objection' certificate within his administrative area, how can he be trusted with the lives of thousands of soldiers under battle conditions? Eminent journalist Karan Thapar in his interview with Gen Deepak Kapoor has mentioned that this is a case of official impropriety and not corruption. Differences between higher officials should not be aired in public, as is being done today. The criterion of judgment should be bona-fides of the decision taken. If the Commanding Officers have to look over their shoulders for instructions in matters which fall within their jurisdiction, the same situation will prevail under battle conditions. Over exposure of the armed forces to public glare through the media will undermine their discipline and will lead to leakage of vital information to the enemy. If an atmosphere of distrust and witchhunt is created within the armed forces, it will be suicidal for the country.

Liberalization and Corruption

While liberalization (opening up the economy to global casino capitalism) has created billionaires and millionaires galore, it has also opened up floodgates of corruption. A huge parallel economy has grown side by side with the corporate sector and is functioning outside the purview of the state machinery, with minimum of publicity. These people have become a law unto themselves and have been able to take full advantage of the loopholes in the Indian laws. The Government agencies failure to charge-sheet Hasan Ali, although he is suspected to have been involved in antinational activities like gun running and money laundering, is a classic example of this. He has also the dubious distinction of being the highest income tax defaulter, with dues running into more than Rs. 60,000 crores. Cases have been under investigation against him since at least 2006 without any tangible result. The Swiss government refused to give any information on his bank accounts on the letter rogatory of the Government of India. Ostensible reason was that the failure to file tax returns is not an offence under Swiss laws and the supporting documents were forged. Tax havens like Switzerland have at no time helped in tracing the trail of black money, for the simple reason that their economy is dependent on the same. Their laws are so tailored that their banks can avoid giving any information on transactions and their sources. While economic globalization is being speeded up, laws of different countries are different. Economic globalization can be successful, only with uniform tax laws and banking regulations. Low tax regime countries are attracting unaccounted money from India, leading to huge tax evasions amongst other more serious crimes.

Dubious banking and financial institutions in the Middle East, particularly Dubai (playground of rich and powerful) have led to Hawala and other money laundering operations in a massive scale. The Government agencies have little or no knowledge of these massive financial operations. Hawala system has a network of brokers spread over different countries. It is a parallel banking system, without any documentation, operating from Dubai, which has different banking laws from India. Switzerland and Great Britain are also important conduits for hawala funds. Although hawala operations violate Indian banking and other laws and have been going on openly since the gulf boom, nothing tangible has been done to check it by the government. Operating without any documents, these operations are important tools for money laundering and funding terrorist activities within the country. In fact the first step to make money laundering illegal was taken by enactment of Prevention of Money Laundering Act in 2002, but strangely it was not implemented immediately and came into force only in July 2005.

Chasing the trail of black money is fraught with red herrings at every stage. In the meantime, the hawala operators are able to transfer the unaccounted money from one account to the other. Dilatory tactics by the Swiss authorities enabled Hasan Ali to transfer huge amount of unaccounted money to undisclosed source, thus throwing a red herring before Indian government agencies. This shows that a person out to sabotage the legal system can always do so by staying one step ahead of the state enforcement authorities. These people with their ill-gotten wealth can mobilize the best legal and financial services to bail them out. People have a secret admiration for individuals, who can twist the law in their favour. Media could hardly hide its glee, when the Mumbai court granted bail to Hasan Ali and blamed the Enforcement Agency for not having any documentary evidence against him. As the Hawala transactions are conducted without any legal instruments, it is well nigh impossible to prove the trail of black money in a court of law. Custodial interrogation has also become out of fashion, mainly from the ever increasing pressure from the mushrooming human rights lobbies. Courts are also reluctant to grant the same, as happened in the Hasan Ali case, although the Supreme Court was convinced that a crime has been committed. Subsequently, Supreme Court set aside the order of the lower court, but the time gained by the accused could have been used for manipulating the records. There are obviously many such clandestine financial empires, as the estimates of black money, both inside and outside the country indicate. Existing legal system, based on documentary evidence, is not in a position to tackle the problem. Simply politicizing the issue and blaming the government machinery for being flat footed will not address the problem. A great Indian blame game is going on parallel to the game of cricket. Both are legacies of our colonial past. It is necessary that various organs of the state cooperate and coordinate with each other instead of indulging in turf war.

Failure of the state to prevent the growth of a huge parallel economy shows that our legal system has sufficient loopholes to allow the main players to escape the tax net, as also indulge in Hawala transactions and money laundering. A clever criminal with his one step ahead of the law strategy, can do enough damage to the economy, before he is apprehended. Parallel economy runs side by side with the regular economy and it is difficult to distinguish one from the other. The Satyam fiasco is a glaring example of how a company with international standing and with reputed persons in the board of directors, could siphon off company funds with impunity over the years. Barons of the parallel economy do not have a board of directors answerable to anyone but themselves. They are not bothered by maintenance of regular accounts or audits (these were of no use even with reputed auditors, in the cases of Satyam and Enron).

The state governments are also seriously mired in the problems of corruption. In Maharastra, Chief Minister, Ashok Chavan had to resign under pressure from the Congress high command, in the wake of the Adarsh housing scam. In Congress Party, the system of high command is there since the days of Mahatma Gandhi. In Karnataka, a running battle is going on between the BJP Chief Minister and the Governor, a Congressman, on the issue of corruption. This is considerably affecting the administration of the state. In states like Orisa and Tamil Nadu, which have regional parties in government, the Chief Ministers are also party heads and do not have to look behind their shoulders. In Tamil Nadu, Karunanidhi and his daughter, Kanimozhi openly supported the blemished Telecom Minister, A. Raja. It is unlikely that without the support of the DMK Supremo, Raja would have ventured into such blatant acts of irregularities and corruption.

The Orissa government has also its fair share of corruption problems. Chief Minister, Naveen Patnaik joined politics after the death of his father, Biju Patnaik to carry on his legacy. It was a case of political succession. Since joining politics, he has been continuously in government, first as Union Minister and then as Central Minister. He has been electorally the most successful Chief Minister, having secured three successive terms, which none of his predecessors could do. He has not come up from the political milieu and did not carry a political baggage, being new to politics. Janata Party leaders in Orissa, with a tradition of working under a dominant supremo like Biju Patnaik and with their own differences, thought it best to have a non-political person from the Biju family, as their titular head. However, once Naveen Patnaik was in the seat of power, there was no looking back for him. He got rid of the over-ambitious leaders in the party one by one. One of the reasons for his success in election is the fact that people do not prefer the traditional politician. He had been able to maintain his clean image in public till lately, by sacking ministers, when there are complaints of corruption against them. This also gave him the opportunity to sack inconvenient persons. However, three major scams have surfaced, which cannot be simply put to the misdeeds of a few ministers. Irregularities in the implementation of National Rural Employment Guarantee Scheme (since named after Mahatma Gandhi, perhaps as a talisman against corruption), have led to complaints from various NGOs. Comptroller & Auditor General in his report has pointed to serious irregularities in the implementation of the scheme, particularly in the backward regions of the state. Lack of coordination between the Centre and the state is one of the main reasons for corruption in the implementation of the scheme. The Supreme Court has asked for a CBI probe into the matter. But the entire matter has strong political undertones, as the ruling party functionaries may be cornering a substantial portion of the funds to build their vote banks.

General preference for a non-career politician, also explains the reason for success of Dr Manmohan Singh, at least till the flood of corruptions hit the UPA government. He could come out clean from the major Securities scam (popularly known as Harshad Mehta scam) of the nineties, when he was the Union Finance Minister. According to the Parliamentary system of government, responsibility for such a massive scam is that of the Minister and the Cabinet. During the NDA rule also, scams like UTI scam, which affected millions of shareholders, did not lead to the Finance Minister or the Cabinet owning up any responsibility. In the financial jungle created after liberalization, scams are the order of the day and the Governments do not lose too much of sleep over these.

Reports of scams are the order of the day and are threatening to discredit almost all the institutions of the country. This has led to loss of public trust and everybody is suspicious of others. In such a situation, development of the country is hardly possible. It is a good sign that the Supreme Court is taking a proactive role in the matter of corruption. The 2G scam and the Radiia tapes have opened up the eyes of the public to the anatomy of corruption, where ministers, secretaries, politicians, media and corporate houses are all involved, either directly or indirectly. It is necessary to break this unholy nexus. Previously a case of bribery or corruption used to involve two individuals, viz., bribe giver and bribe taker and was a case of aberration. But this is no longer the case now. Corruption today is a much more complex issue and has taken the shape of an organized crime. Telecom scams right from Sukh Ram to A Raja are clear indicators of these. Scams are also due to the wrong policies pursued by successive governments. Supreme Court, being prima facie convinced, has ordered probe right from 2001, when the new telecom policy came into effect. Telecom sector has been opened up too fast and in a hurry, without any concern for national security. Leasing of communication channels to parties with doubtful credentials is undoubtedly a security threat. Immediate cause of highlighting the 2G scam is the blatant role of Raja and his supporters in favouring parties with doubtful credentials like DB Reality floated Swan Telecom. But now, it is apparent that lot of big names of the corporate world are involved. Criminal activities have come in the open, mostly due to the custodial enquiry of Raja and his Assistants. Shivraj Patil Committee has brought out number of irregularities in granting of telecom licenses since 2003. Merely the fact that it was granted to an established party, does not absolve the government of the charges of irregularity. It is necessary to go into the bottom of the problem to find out the level of corruption in the country and the various parties involved. Favouring party by itself is a corrupt practice, whether immediate benefit through bribery is involved or not. In the present scenario, many professionals and politicians have close relations with corporate houses as advisors and consultants. It is easy to have a quid pro quo, when one is in power. It is necessary to bring out the nexus between politicians, bureaucrats, corporate houses, media, sundry power brokers and professionals, without the connivance of whom corruption in such a large scale is not possible. Joint Parliamentary Committee is a step in the right direction, as it is not possible for a police agency like CBI to probe into the entire matter, which goes well beyond the traditional concept of criminality.

Corruption today is not an individual crime, but is a well organized affair and has become a part of the system. Recent 2G scam involving ex-Minister Raja and a few others is only a miniscule portion of the tip of the proverbial iceberg. Policies suiting different corporate houses have been followed right from the inception of the telecom boom, particularly from 2000. Justice Shivraj Patil Committee Report reveals the lack of transparency and arbitrariness in issue of licenses since that time. Swings in policy to suit parties of choice are apparent. There is scant regard for official procedure. Private Secretaries are putting up notes on behalf of the Ministers. There are no interdepartmental consultations, as is required under rules of business. Ministers have been pursuing their own agenda in complete disregard of the official procedures. In such a situation, the official machinery has been turned into a mere rubber stamp. Selected corporate houses are given favoured treatment and there is undue haste in pushing through their cases. Justice Patil Committee Report, which is based on documents, clearly shows that this has been going on since 2001. Documents do not lie and since these matters are in public domain, one can draw one's conclusion from the same. Prime Minister's statement that Mr. Raja has been following the NDA government's policy does not seem to be wrong.

If Raja was following the well established policy of his predecessors, where did he go wrong? Obviously, Raja coming from the backwaters of Tamil Nadu, stretched his luck too far. Had he been more media savvy, this calamity might not have befallen him. He had also too many political masters to serve. Being comparatively new to the Delhi circuit, he was caught up in the crossfire between different corporate houses. It is well known that business rivals find a convenient scapegoat in politicians and bureaucrats. Only a business rival will take the trouble of finding out, which party has got an undue advantage and at what price. Whistleblowers are more likely to get their information from disgruntled parties, who have their own axe to grind. Raja was a man in a hurry with the forthcoming elections in view and went for short term gain, instead of long term relationship. Obviously in the process, he did not fail to enrich himself and his extended family. One of the few important factors, which emerge from the recent revelations in the wake of 2G scam, is the important role corporate houses are playing in the government system. Close relationship between the corporates and the Government is one of the significant developments of the post-liberalistion scenario. This is the new pattern of democracy and is closer to the American system. In such a scenario, grassroot politicians with electoral constituencies to take care of, will be at a considerable disadvantage. In a political career designed to build a local electoral base, they are unlikely to be media or corporate savvy. Mass-based politicians are gradually becoming out of fashion and are being sidelined by self styled professionals and experts. This was certainly not the intention of the democratic polity envisaged in the Constitution. Let us hope that we are not sliding from Licence Control Raj to Corporate Raj.

Chapter – III

Myth of British Administration and its Legacy

As a throwback of the colonial legacy, it is still widely believed that the Britishers had given a strong and efficient administrative structure to the country and Indian Civil Service was the steel frame, which held this structure together. The memoirs and reports of the British officers give an impression that they found a lawless country and brought order in a chaotic situation. We have enough historical evidence to show that even before the advent of the British our villages had well-developed Panchayats to adjudicate in village disputes. The Panchayati system, which had evolved over generations, was largely left undisturbed by the Muslim rulers. Major crimes were very uncommon, as the value system and the societal influence acted as a check. 'A general consideration of the outstanding features of the Hindu revenue system, tends to show that the Indian system of revenue administration, far from being slight and primitive may claim to have surpassed the achievements of classical antiquity as well as medieval Europe and even anticipated some of the broad characteristics of modern finance.'[1]

Baden Powell, an eminent authority on Indian land administration system writes that under the earlier Indian system "the revenue demand was not enforced except in the most elastic manner and that pressure was relaxed at once in a bad season".[2] The European principle was punctual and inexorable payment, with no scope for relaxation, even in bad years and was more impersonal and rule-bound, with no in-built flexibility to adjust according to the vagaries of nature.

The Indian system was based on the principle that a satisfied peasantry assured of their land rights, is fundamental to a sustainable agrarian economy and forms the basis of good governance. Even, before the Muslim conquest, India had a well developed land administration system, which survived through a greater part of that rule. It was not that there were no exploitation of the peasantry from time to time, but the basic principles of land administration continued to be sound. "All settled rulers have recognized that security to the cultivators means in the long run the best revenue".[3] The Muslim rulers, basically being herdsmen from the Asian Steppes and not accustomed to settled cultivation, had little idea of land administration in an agrarian system. They were too happy to let the existing system largely untouched. "Many of the institutions of ancient India, far from being swept away by the shock of the Muslim conquest, actually released a new lease of life after that catastrophe".[4]

Revenue collection being farmed out to contractors was altogether new to the Indian system and was introduced for the first time by the British administration towards the end of the eighteenth century. The concept of an intermediary between cultivators and the State, which is best known as a tool of exploitation, was alien to India. Parliament of Great Britain at that time was an Assembly of Landlords. The policy makers were acquainted with only the system in their own country and had no knowledge of the Indian system, which had evolved over centuries. They created a system in which the tax collectors became landlords with absolute ownership of land and the rights of the peasants were placed at the whims of the former.

The Government in its eagerness to increase the revenue collection destroyed the earlier system, where the cultivators had full rights over their land and was not at the mercy of an intermediary. The policy makers assuaged their conscience with the glib notion that the British collectors will be in place to safeguard the interests of the cultivators, not realizing the impossibility of such a task. After taking away the rights of the cultivators, they were placed under a distant Godfather (British collector). The notion was that a single trained British officer imbued with an imperial zeal can do wonders in a huge district, inhabited by the natives, who have been denuded of their basic rights of ownership of their cultivable land. The land policy changed the socio-economic structure of the provinces, where they were introduced. This is the beginning of dependency theory, where the native population, denuded of their rights, is made to depend on the foreign master for its very sustenance. Even primitive societies have basic laws to manage their affairs and complete super imposition of an alien system will result in the disintegration of that society.

India, at the advent of British rule certainly cannot be considered to be an uncivilized country by any stretch of imagination. Even a common sense view would indicate that a populous sub-continent like India, could not have managed to survive for such a long time without a basic administrative system. The system was certainly not perfect, as no system devised by men, is ever perfect. Administrative system is more a matter of evolution than imposition from above. The fundamental of administration is local self-governance and a government run by central dictat, is unlikely to be effective. The corner-stone of the administrative system was racial superiority, where "A young Englishman sent to India to be a part of the covenanted civil service would belong to a class whose national dominance over each and every Indian was absolute".[5] This was the mindset of the administrative system, which we inherited lock, stock and barrel.

The concept of the Indian Civil Service (ICS) is firmly rooted in this idea. The British administrators, particularly the ICS had the white man's burden as a baggage to contend with. Even after part indigenization of the ICS, this theory continued, albeit in an indirect form. A few Indians could aspire to reach the level of white men and be admitted to the charmed circle. The policy of admitting a few Indians of merit, who satisfied their criteria and could play the game according to the rules laid down by them, was a clever ploy of the Empire. However, one of the earliest entrants to the ICS, Romesh Chandra Dutt became a severe critic of the colonial system of government and after taking early retirement from the service, wrote several books on the subject severely criticizing the British administration, particularly their policy towards the peasantry and their subtle exploitation of the economy of the country.[6]

Sudden imposition of an alien system resulted in the disintegration of the existing socio-economic structure. After demolishing the existing administrative system, the Britishers tried to impose a new system in their own way. This system did not recognize the existing self-governing institutions like village panchayats, which had been the basis of administration in the villages. The image conceived was one of changeless Indian village and despotism. In fact, it had deep distrust of the same and considered it to be a source of oriental exploitation. The Britishers were keen to protect the Indians from the Indians themselves and assumed the so-called Whiteman's Burden. They proceeded to administer India in their own light. The fundamental to this system, was the distrust of the Indians and their exclusion from all higher government posts. 'Statements like "The Hindu is inherently untruthful and lacks moral courage" were expressions of wisdom from which very few, least of all the governors of Bengal dissented; similarly, when a historian of India like Sir HM Elliot planned his work, central to it was the notion of Indian barbarity'.[7] There are plenty of such gems of wisdom, which were not accidental statements or loose talks, but firmly held beliefs and the basis of the administrative system.

Great Britain's primary aim in establishing a colony in India was to have a huge farmland to support their manufacturing activities in the home country. Certainly, they had not suddenly been fired at a particular time in history by an overwhelming missionary zeal to civilize the entire world. Agriculture, which had always been a way of life for the people, besides being the source of economic sustenance, was commercialized to produce cash crops like indigo, cotton and jute to provide raw materials for industrial revolution in Britain. Marketing was controlled by the government and commercialization of agriculture did not benefit the peasantry, as is seen from the fact that per capita income decreased during the British rule.

Colonizers sincerely believed that they had brought an ordered administrative system in a country, where such concepts were non-existent. The administration in their own country during the period, when they were busy building up their colonial empire was far from desirable. The civil service of Great Britain of the nineteenth century was a patronage one and referred to as "a gigantic system of outdoor relief system of the British aristocracy", in the House of Commons by the great liberal politician, John Bright, who had become a political institution of his time. There are number of studies bringing out the pathetic state of affairs in the British civil service.[8] Bungling nature of British bureaucracy has also been portrayed by famous novelists of the time. Anthony Trollope has portrayed the situation half humorously in his novel 'The Three Clerks.' Charles Dickens's famous or notorious "circumlocution office"[9] in his novel 'Little Dorritt', brings out the injustice being meted out to the common citizens by an indifferent, self-perpetuating, insular bureaucracy, where everybody is related in some way or the other, right up to the top. The speciality of this form of bureaucracy is passing the buck, where nobody takes the responsibility, against a jumble of rules and regulations.

Britain of the industrial revolution was an economic and social paradox. While Britain had become a rich country and a few had become exceedingly rich, majority of people had become poor. Commercialisation of agriculture resulted in large-scale displacement of peasantry. Industry could accommodate a small portion of these people and majority was reduced to utter poverty. State had to intervene and 'Poor Laws' came into existence. The administration of these laws was exceedingly bad, with rampant corruption. The matter had been raised several times in the Parliament, with demand to scrap them, as wastage of public money. British Parliament, the citadel of democracy, was more concerned with the wastage of public money to provide relief to the poor, than administering them in a better way. This clearly shows the class composition of the British Parliament of the time.

A Royal Commission was appointed in 1832 to inquire into the working of Poor Law. 'The report of the Commission drew attention to the abuses which had grown up, the pauperisation of labourers, the abuse of the system by employers, the corruption and incapacity of officials, the carelessness with which outdoor relief was granted by the Justices over the heads of their subordinates, the disadvantageous position of the independent and self-respecting labourer, and the particular abuses associated with the workhouse.'[10] One would expect that the Report of the Commission would stir the collective conscience of the nation and immediate steps taken to improve the administration of the system. But the result was opposite and the Poor Law Amendment Act of 1834, shirked away the responsibility of the State of maintaining those, who are not able to maintain themselves.

The Amended Act 'did nothing to reduce the amount of poverty, and it failed to recognise any obligation upon the community to provide work for those who needed it and were willing to do it'.[11] This was *laissez faire* in the extreme, where 'every one for oneself and devil take the hindmost'. Certainly, this was not the philosophy of Adam Smith, who was first and foremost a moral scientist. (His earlier publication was 'Theory of Moral Sentiments', 1759). A wonderful situation indeed, in the mid-nineteenth century, when Britain was at the peak of the Empire and had taken up the mission of civilizing the entire world! British genius was more suited to rule over colonies, where people were subjugated and they were the masters.

We would have expected that things would have changed for the better, after the passing away of the conservative Victorian era and Britain's dalliance with socialism, under successive Labour Governments. Immediately after the Second World War, the Labour Party was elected with a huge majority under the mandate from the electorate to take up major welfare programmes and launch a drive for nationalisation of industries. It was a Government with persons, having high credentials in socialism and life time experience in labour movements and they meant business in implementing their given agenda. A few years earlier visualizing such a situation, when the Labour Party wins the elections with a clear mandate, HJ Laski, the famous political scientist and socialist had predicted a violent upheaval between the conservative elements of the society and the forces of socialism.[12] He was of the view that in such a situation, bureaucracy would squarely be on the side of the conservatives by flatly refusing to function under a socialist government and thus fuel the fires of revolution, which had engulfed many of the countries. British bureaucracy did nothing of the kind and functioned as usual under the new regime, proving Professor Laski, a false prophet of doom. This earned the bureaucracy high accolades, as a sign of maturity and neutrality.

Bureaucratic neutrality became synonymous with British bureaucracy and a model for newly independent countries. Leaders of most countries thought that, if only they had a similar pattern of bureaucracy, they could have transmitted their programme into action. Britain, indeed was fortunate in having such a self-effacing and neutral administrative personnel eager to function under any regime. As we will see, this was simply a ploy to contain the socialist policies of the Labour government and to ensure the continuance of the existing socio-economic system.

The high moral tone adopted by the British bureaucrats should have been found disconcerting to an impartial observer. A person, who has no personal views of his own and can serve any master willingly, for his own upkeep, will be a rarity indeed. Such a person can only be found in the fictional character of the Butler, Jeeves in PG Wodehouse's novels.[13] The newly independent countries, however fell for this model and started training their newly inducted bureaucrats accordingly. Neutrality of the bureaucracy became the watchword and lucky ones were also deputed abroad to induct this ethos and model themselves on British bureaucrats. Britain was, however, too eager to train up our higher bureaucracy and various training schemes were accordingly formulated. High moral tone of the British bureaucracy was in fact an exercise in real politic, of which even the great Italian philosopher like Machiavelli would have been proud. They knew that the Parliament and the ministers will have to implement their policies through the bureaucracy and there lies the crux of the matter.

The Government's policies have to be made workable for implementation and this is the work of higher level bureaucracy, whereas actual execution is the job of lower level bureaucracy. Labour Party agenda envisaged a vastly increased role of the administrative machinery and this led to its large-scale increase at all levels. Bureaucracy saw an increasing role for itself under the new dispensation and a consequent scope for unprecedented expansion. Parkinson's books on bureaucracy, which are based on facts and thorough research, give a detailed account of the British bureaucracy of that period. In fact, Parkinson's Law or how the bureaucracy perpetuates itself became synonymous with the ever expanding bureaucracy of modern times.[14] India has faithfully followed the British model and has not lagged behind in the expansion of bureaucracy on a much larger scale.

The Labour government of post-war Britain was happy to have a cooperative bureaucracy, which immediately took to the task of implementation of its socialistic programme. Results of the socialistic experiment through the bureaucracy were far from encouraging and many of the schemes were bogged down in various official bottlenecks. Delivery system faced serious problems due to the wide reach of the scheme and was not entirely satisfactory. There were serious complaints on the quality of service provided by the government operated National Health Service, which was envisaged to bring health services to all. In actual practice, those, who could not afford any better health service, opted for nationalised health service, while those who could afford better medical services, went elsewhere. The scheme, although continuing, has been highly weakened.

Even the comparatively simpler project of supplying free milk to primary school students from lower income groups, ran into difficulties, due to large-scale mismanagement and pilferage, leading to the abolition of the scheme altogether by the newly inducted Secretary for Education, Margaret Thatcher in the early seventies. This earned her the acronym 'Thatcher, the milk snatcher'. It did her no harm and firmly established her conservative credentials, paving the way for her shortly taking up the leadership of the Conservative Party and eventually becoming the Prime Minister. Thatcher did not try to improve the delivery system, but instead used the alibi of mismanagement and corruption to do away with a socially useful scheme.

Failure of the policies of Labour government, paved the way for the emergence of the new right, best illustrated by the policies of Margaret Thatcher. In fact, there was a complete U-turn in both ideology and policy. This situation continued with the Labour government under Tony Blair, which had shed all socialistic pretensions. It is a matter of conjecture, whether socialistic policies failed due to their inherent weaknesses or due to administrative bottlenecks and mismanagement. But the bureaucracy certainly had a major role in such a failure. It would have been better to point out the shortcomings of the policies at an appropriate time, so that corrective measures could have been taken.

The fact emerges that it is easier to be rulers than administrators. There is obviously distinction between ruling and administration and one has to be kept distinct from the other. In case of rulers, subordination of the people is assured, not so in the case of administrators. During foreign rule, even the lowest functionary is a ruler, by virtue of deriving his authority from the foreign master. The position changed overnight with the advent of independence, when people gave themselves self-governance. The rulers were overnight converted into administrators.

Administering ones own country is much more difficult, than ruling over subjects. Britain administered their own country through a jumble of rules and regulations, where justice, although theoretically available, was completely elusive. Charles Dickens's novels, which are the best available mirrors of his time, vividly portray the scandalous state of administration in the country. Most of his novels deal with the harassment meted out to ordinary citizens by corrupt lower level government officials like Rent Collectors, officials in charge of poor houses and such others. While corrupt officials were let free to harass common citizens on paltry and often trumped up matters, there was no redress available from any quarters and their reports were treated to be sacrosanct. Punishments for minor transgression of laws were unduly harsh and unjust. For failure to pay rent in time, one could expect to find oneself in the debtors' prison for a life time.

The higher bureaucracy functioned in a make-belief world of its own, where nobody takes any responsibility and is busy feathering his own nest. Dickens has outlined the working of the higher bureaucracy in the chapter 'Containing the Whole Science of Government' in 'Little Dorrit', which is certainly a study of public administration of his time, with fictional characters. Circumlocution Office (an imaginary government department), which was manned by righteous individuals, with a high sense of public probity, was the main department to keep any questioning public in their proper place. The department was open to the public and never turned down anybody. Its method was simple enough. It referred a person from one office to the other and then back again. It had perfected this little game and its motto was 'How Not to Do It?. The Department had established the complete Rule of Law and had made the ordinary citizens of Britain submit and acquiesce to any high handedness by the minions of law, meekly. General demoralisation of the lower middle class and the working class form the backdrop of Dickens's novels. Of course, they had the consolation that they belonged to a master race and were superior to the colonial people. During the nineteenth century, when Britain was busy governing an empire, it failed to administer its own backyard.

India today is passing through a similar phase of industrial revolution, which Britain experienced in the nineteenth century. Similarities are all too obvious. English school of economists had formulated their policies in the light of their experience of industrial revolution. After India was liberated from foreign rule, we wanted to replicate the British experiment of industrialisation. This has led to high level of growth and modernisation and equally high level of poverty, as in the case of Britain of the nineteenth century. Socio-economic structure is in the melting pot of industrial revolution and a new structure is emerging. Will it be a better one? The developing scenario does not suggest so. In Human Development Index (covering 180 United Nations member states), prepared by United Nations Development Programme and released on October, 2009 India ranks at 129, well below countries like China, Sri Lanka and Indonesia.[15] According to the Global Hunger Index for the year 2009, prepared by International Food Policy Research Institute for 84 countries in Asia, Africa and South America, where hunger was a major problem in 1990, India ranks 65th, with only Bangladesh (67th) and Yemen (74th) for company in Asia. China ranks 5th and North Korea (where according to the US, famine conditions are prevailing) ranks 46th. Immediate neighbouring countries like Sri Lanka rank at 45, with Myanmar at 53.[16] There has been slowdown and near stagnation of poverty rates in India since 1992, whereas Bangladesh has made significant progress in this regard. The problem of food shortage is likely to become more serious, with the Director General of FAO sounding a global warning.

Whatever development India has achieved in the last decade and half, it has certainly not been in the field of poverty alleviation. Economic theories practised today are geared to increase the number of rich, while simultaneously increasing the number of absolute poor. Indian state cannot afford to follow a *laissez faire* policy as was followed by Britain in their industrial development, for the simple reason that we do not have colonies of emigration like Australia, New Zealand, Canada, South Africa, etc. Britain could safely siphon off their surplus population to their newly acquired colonies. We do not have such luxury of a colonial empire. Germany tried the British pattern of industrialisation in the last century and ended up with two World Wars.

In view of the above mentioned situation, Indian State will have to go in for more and more anti-poverty programmes, to support those falling behind in the rat race of job-less economic growth. A Darwinian situation is developing fast, which is beyond the control of *laissez faire* economics (free market economics). There is no doubt that the economic forces let loose in the last few years have created severe dispossession, the major sign of which is large-scale urban migration, leading to creation of unauthorised slums in urban areas. We cannot afford to shy away from this situation, which the British society did in the nineteenth century. The State will have to devise more and more poverty alleviation and anti-hunger schemes, as well take more proactive role in their implementation, in the years to come. Ways and means have to be devised to that end and larger amount of funds have to be allotted to meet this growing problem.

Concept of All India Services

When the British were leaving India in 1947, things were quite different from earlier times. Communal violence, which preceded independence, led to a civil war situation and the partition of the country. In such a situation, leaders of the independence movement rightly decided not to disturb the existing administrative structure, when they took over control of administration from the British Raj. The Indian Civil Service, due to its high profile and visibility, was considered to be the kingpin of administrative system. Besides, many of the top leaders of the independence movement, particularly the first Prime Minister of independent India, Jawaharlal Nehru, knew many of the ICS Officers, from his student days in England. This helped the ICS officers, who had the same background as Nehru, in establishing a close rapport with him. In view of these, both Nehru and Vallabh Bhai Patel, the Deputy Prime Minister and the Home Minister, decided to continue with the ICS, with the same terms and conditions of service, as they were enjoying under the British Crown. There were serious reservations about continuance of the ICS, in its pre-independence colonial form, by some of the leaders, notably C Rajagopalachari. Rank and file of the Congress Party was also not in favour of this. However, both Nehru and Patel overruled these objections and ICS became the premier government service in independent India.

The leaders of the country particularly the Prime Minister and the Deputy Prime Minister were concerned with the fissiparous tendencies, which had surfaced in different parts of the country and their primary aim was to maintain the integrity of the country. With this in mind, they were in favour of a superior administrative and police services, owing allegiance to the Centre. All India Administrative and Police Services were conceived on the model of the ICS and IP (Indian Police). As in the case of ICS, where the appointing authority was the Secretary of State for India in the British cabinet, in the case of IAS the appointing authority was the Governor General and subsequently President, after the Constitution came into effect. Immediately after independence, IAS was constituted and an emergency recruitment taken up, with a limited examination and an interview. Regular recruitment to the IAS was taken up from 1948 onwards.

IAS was thus the successor service of the ICS and was conceived for giving continuity to the administrative system. IAS inherited the same value system as the ICS, as the former were trained by the latter or had them as their official superiors. The ICS officers were certainly efficient, but their value system was a colonial one, with an attitude, which varied from patronizing to open distrust of the subordinates. It was impossible for an ICS officer to treat a subordinate as equal. This was not a good start for a democratic system. Memoirs of the ICS officers give the impression that they had come to rule over a lawless and corrupt society and most of the subordinates were corrupt and untrustworthy. Only the fear of the District Magistrate kept them at check. It is obvious that they had little faith in their subordinates. However, they could not distrust everybody and had to depend on somebody. This gave rise to a small coterie of people, who were the eyes and ears of the District Magistrate. They were also the advisers of the authority. This is certainly not a healthy system. Steps should have been taken to restructure the bureaucracy at the very beginning of transfer of power. The administrative system, which we inherited, was designed to prop up the imperial system and not suitable for a democratic country.

The IAS officers were to work in a different system altogether, where the power was with the politicians, who were responsible to the legislature and their constituency. The parallelism with ICS was incompatible in a democratic system. The mode of administration in pre-independence India was not at all suitable for a democratic country. The result was an unseemly tug of war for power between the politicians and the bureaucrats, with the latter flaunting their knowledge of rules and regulations, whereas the former their authority as the primacy of the political executive. This is certainly not a healthy atmosphere, resulting in a free for all situations. Both the politicians and bureaucrats, being ambitious individuals, try to increase their sphere of influence by various means. The result is a power game, where those bureaucrats, who are able to extend their sphere of influence, prosper. In a power system, one has to be close to real source of power and there lies the art of bureaucratic salvation. This creates a huge system of patronage, which is not good for a democratic developmental country.

IAS was designated All India Service, because the officers of this service can be called upon to serve both in the Centre and the state. It was also expected that, since the Central Government was the appointing authority of these officers, their loyalty would be to the Centre, rather than the state. This, in fact created serious problem, as some of the state Chief Ministers did not take kindly to this approach and considered it to be a breach of state autonomy. However, since all the Chief Ministers, after independence were from the Congress Party and Nehru and Patel were their supreme leaders, they acquiesced in this, rather unwillingly. This was an inauspicious start for a new service. The dual control envisaged over the All Indian Service, was not a feasible one. Since the IAS officers are called upon to serve in the states and are allotted to state cadres, the arbiter of their service conditions is the respective state government, which is the cadre controlling authority. The Central Government has little or no control, over transfer, postings, promotions, assessment and other service conditions of these officers. Although the cadre for the Union Territories is controlled by the Ministry of Personnel of the Central Government, the bulk of the IAS officers are fully under the control of the respective state governments. However, the personnel department of the Government of India keeps a duplicate copy of the service records of the officers. Any representation against the order of the state government is rare and unlikely to succeed, as the Central Government is generally reluctant to interfere in the action of the state government in a service matter, in the name of state autonomy. In rare cases, where this happens, it is only due to the clout of the officer either political or administrative in the Central Government.

In view of the foregoing facts, the nomenclature "All India Service" is a misnomer. IAS is basically a superior State Service, where the selection is made by the Union Public Service Commission on an all India basis and initial appointment and placement are made by the Central Government. The reason for the name 'All India Service' was based on the clause that IAS officers might be called upon to serve the Central Government. This clause, however, is not mandatory and is only enabling. The cadre controlling authority, the State Government is well within its power, not to spare a particular officer on Central deputation. An IAS officer works under the Central Government on deputation, with the consent of the state government. It is possible for officers of Central Services and even state services, to go on deputation to the Central Government, with the consent of their cadre controlling authorities. As such, there is nothing unique about IAS officers being sent on Central deputation. The foregoing position will be equally applicable to the other two All India Services like the IPS (Indian Police Service) and IFS (Indian Forest Service).

Central deputation is highly selective and there are no well-laid down guidelines for this. Unless an officer has some connections in the Central Government, it is difficult to go on deputation. It has generally been seen that officers from outside the State are keen to go on deputation at an early stage of their service career, as they feel they have better chance of career advancement in the Central Government. The insiders are not so keen to go on Central deputation at the early stage, but would like to go on Central deputation at a later stage of their service career, as prize posts are available under the Centre at that stage. It is necessary to have a proper system of deputation, in which all the officers have a fair chance of working in the Central Government and show their merit. The present system of deputation does injustice to lot of officers without political or administrative clout and is demoralizing. There is also no system of representation against this practice.

Endnotes

1. UN Ghoshal, *Contributions to the History of The Hindu Revenue System,* Second Edition, 1972, p.362, Saraswat Library, Calcutta. First edition of the book was published by the Calcutta University in 1929.
2. Baden Powell, *The Indian Village Community,* p.209n, quoted in ibid, p.382.
3. Baden Powell, ibid, p.209n.
4. UN Ghoshal, ibid, p.378.

5. Edward W. Said, *Culture and Imperialism,* Vintage Books, New York, 1994, p.151.
6. Romesh C Dutt was one of the earliest Indian entrants to the Indian Civil Service and was the first to rise to the rank of a Commissioner. His experience in high administrative offices, made him see the true character of British imperialism and its effect on the Indian economy. However, his claim to fame does not rest merely on his administrative achievements. He was one of the pioneers in launching a powerful intellectual war against the wrong policies and mismanagement of the British Government, which resulted in repeated famines and created hardships to common people. The true value of intellectual struggle in our freedom movement is not perhaps realized and only political struggle is given importance. However, there can be no political movement, without a sound theoretical base. Dutt exhibited rarest of rare courage in taking on the mighty British Empire, particularly its pompous representative, Lord Curzon. This is all the more so for a person, who had served the government in high administrative post. In the pantheon of freedom fighters, Dutt ranks amongst the highest.

   British Government did not take any punitive action against Dutt and left it to the Viceroy, Lord Curzon to fend off Dutt's attack. Not content with Curzon's rebuttal of his arguments, Dutt took up the matter with the Secretary of State for India, Lord George Hamilton. British Empire well realized that any punitive action against Dutt would have the effect of turning him into a martyr against British imperialism and they were keen to deny him the halo of a martyr.
7. Edward Said, *Culture and Imperialism,* p.151.
8. Frederic A Ogg and Harold Zink, *Modern Foreign Governments,* Macmillan Company, New York, 1957, p.140.
9. Charles Dickens, *Little Dorrit,* Collins, London, 1962, p.108-126.
10. George W. Southgate, *English Economic History,* JM Dent and Sons Ltd, London, 1960, p.285.
11. Ibid, p.286.
12. HJ Laski, *Democracy in Crisis,* George Allen & Unwin Ltd, London, 1944.

13. Jeeves is the typical English butler portrayed in PG Wodehouse's novels. It is in fact a satire on the British aristocracy and their utter dependence on their retainers.
14. C. Northcote Parkinson, *Parkinson's Law or The Pursuit of Progress,* John Murray, London, 1961.
15. http://upload.wikimedia.org/wikipedia/commons/4/43/Ghi_by_country_700.jpg
16. http://en.wikipedia.org/wiki/List_of_countries_by_Human_Development_Index

Chapter – IV

Bureaucracy is Replica of the Society

Bureaucracy is replica of the society at large. Indian administrative hierarchy nicely replicates the Indian society. Like in the Indian caste system with its numerous castes and sub-castes, the administrative hierarchy consists of numerous tiers of officials. In the administrative set up, you are always below somebody or above somebody. One can always enjoy a vicarious pleasure in the fact that even if one is bullied by the higher echelons, there is somebody else to bully back. This is as good a replica as any of the Indian caste system, coupled with its rigidity of structure. Once one enters the system, one is stuck in a particular groove and has to move within that groove. There are of course circles within circles and even amongst equals, there are some who are considered more equal than the others, due to lack of level playing field. Everybody wants to be before his neighbour, creating a rat race like situation. Concept of inequality is too well entrenched in the Indian psyche, fed on a diet of caste and creed, to be contained by the Preamble to the Constitution, which envisages 'Equality of Status'.

This rigid hierarchical system stifles any attempt at initiative, as anybody speaking out of turn, is likely to offend the boss. If any suggestion is to be given, it must appear, it has emanated from the boss. Under no circumstance, one should give the impression that one is cleverer than the boss. The art of survival in the bureaucracy lies in keeping the boss pleased. The height of perfection in this can be reached by those, who can become an alter ego of the boss. Needless to say this is an art as old as the system of power structure. An individual's success in the administrative hierarchy depends on his proximity to the powers that be.

A power group develops round the boss and there are several tiers of such groups. Beyond these tiers, lies the administrative wilderness, where the vast majority is condemned. This is an exact reflection of the Indian social structure, where the vast majority continues to be underprivileged, whereas a few are in the charmed circle. Administrative inner circle controls the entire bureaucracy. They are, in fact, the most visible part of the system. This practice has become more pronounced in the last few decades. On the plea of cutting through the maze of red-tape, more and more power has been concentrated in the hands of a small group. Over the years, the bureaucratic process has become less and less democratic and more oligarchic.

The system of Committee of Secretaries for quicker decision making, which has been innovated, has in fact eroded the powers of government, which are in charge of individual ministers answerable to Parliament/State Legislative Assembly. This is like another parallel cabinet system for the bureaucracy. Endless meetings and committees have been effective in short-circuiting the system and cutting through a plethora of red tapes. This bureaucratic innovation has been extremely useful in fostering coterie rule. Rules of business, which had been evolved to check the growth of administrative authoritarianism, have been *bid adieu*. Today, the top bureaucrats are more visible than ever before. The days of anonymous public servants are over. The public servants, who matter, are highly visible. This may give an outward appearance of transparency. But one has to be aware of the fact that being available to a section of the press is no guarantee of transparency, rather it may encourage the tendency to play to the gallery.

Over the years, both bureaucrats and politicians have evolved a strategy of mutual co-existence. Today's bureaucrats are as much politicians, as politicians are bureaucrats. The function of one is overlapping the other. The thin dividing line between the role of bureaucracy and politicians is fast disappearing and one is trying to play the other. In fact there is little difference between the role of a politician and a bureaucrat. The official class has the added advantage, in that they do not have to face the electorate and enjoy a permanent tenure. Even retirement is no bar for them, as there are numerous committees and commissions, through which they can carry on their public service. Luckiest ones can go for international assignments, if they have been able to establish enough rapport with the international bodies during their service career. There have been also forays of retired government servants to politics. But, it is interesting to note that their forays are limited to national or state level politics. There has hardly been any attempt on their part to go into grassroot politics, where they would be able to serve the people better.

Inequality - Basis of Colonial Administrative System

Indian culture and tradition has certainly many good points. However, the concept of equality is certainly not one of them. The basic concept is one of subordination. Here by culture/tradition, is meant the basic working value system of the society, which is the engine of the society. When the Britons devised the administrative system, they understood the Indian psyche well and built up the administrative system on this principle, which provided the necessary checks and balances. Plato's ideal of philosopher king is the model on which Britain modelled its administrative system in India. Unlike other conquerors, Britain wanted to administer India, down to the village level and was not satisfied with issuing its fiat from the national or provincial level. Previous rulers were content to let the villages administer themselves. Britain wanted to push their system of administration down to the village level, as part of their policy of economic colonization.

Administering a country of continental proportion by a small island nation, situated thousands of miles overseas in the days of sailing ships was a fantastic idea and could not be possible through superior military power alone. A thorough study of Indian social systems and traditions seems to have been made, before an administrative system was devised for India. It was well understood that respect for wisdom and knowledge has an important place in the Indian psyche. Administrative structure was sought to be built round this concept. This also fell in line with Plato's concept of philosopher king, who must have both these qualities.

This philosopher king has a pre-determined knowledge of good and evil through his communion with the divine. His knowledge is also circumcised by his pre-conceived notion of what is good for the society. 'The philosopher who has communion with the divine' will most likely to be 'overwhelmed by the urge to realize his heavenly vision'. Then again 'philosophical minds always love knowledge of a sort which shows them the eternal nature not varying'.[1] This is a perfect recipe for divine rule of kings and dictators and certainly not conducive to a democratic polity. Moreover such a system abhors any social change towards equality. Dictators from time immemorial have taken their philosophical justification by selling the idea that they alone have a vision of what is good for the society. Plato's experiment in statecraft with philosopher king was a failure even in his own time. Plato's friend and pupil, Dio, who ruled Syracuse on his principles was more a tyrant than an ideal king, according to authentic historical sources.[2]

Plato's society is centred on the concept of natural inequality of men. The clear division is between the ruler and the ruled. In Plato's ideal state, division of labour is based on biological naturalism of inequality. An analysis of Plato's concept of this division is a philosophical and a pseudo-scientific justification of the same. 'The only really important division of labour turns out to be that between rulers and ruled, claimed to be based upon the natural inequality of masters and slaves, of wise and ignorant'.[3] Theoretical justification by the British in putting in place their administrative machinery was found in the Indian social system. 'In India, the caste system was there ready-made and it is odd that the four original castes of the Hindus, corresponds with Plato's'.[4] This comes from a British civilian towards the close of the Empire. Obviously, they understood the Indian caste system well and saw in it an opportunity to fit in their plan of administering a huge empire at a distance of thousands of miles, with a primitive transport system of sailing ships.

It was realised that superior force alone will not be sufficient to keep in control a country of continental size with a large population. There was therefore need for building up an administrative system to fit in with the Indian social psyche. 'The Indian Brahmins of the nineteenth century however were not at all like Plato's guardians; a new caste was needed to complete the state, and the English supplied it. The English Guardians certainly believed there was something in their composition that distinguished them from the people they ruled'.[5] British wanted to fill in the gaps in the existing Indian caste system and gave a new lease of life to this moribund system, which seems to have been in the decline. Long period of Muslim rule had deprived the Brahmins, the opportunity of being spiritual and consequently temporal advisers to the rulers. The new rulers filled in this vacuum.

Continuation of the Colonial Administrative System

We inherited the same system and built up a bureaucratic structure based on subordinates and superiors. The British, who considered themselves to be the masters, had no difficulty in establishing themselves as official superiors. The colonizers were the undoubted masters and the Indians had no difficulty in accepting them as superiors. It is perhaps too much of a coincidence that the four classes in the civil service correspond with the four castes in the Hindu system. Obviously, this was no accident, as the colonial administration wanted to fit in their administrative structure with the Indian social structure. By this, they also created a caste system of their own.

Officials of the covenanted service were supposed to be the Brahmins, whereas the military officers were supposed to be the Khatriyas and the merchant class, the Baniyas. Their protocol system and warrant of precedence are striking evidence of this in the official system. The list of senior office bearers of various elite clubs in India in pre-independence time would clearly indicate the social standing of each of these categories of British personnel in India. Of course, the Indians were in the last category. There was a competition amongst educated Indians to emulate the British, who represented the Master Race. This type of emulation breeds an inferiority complex and is not desirable. This has resulted in a situation, where those who have been educated abroad, particularly in British or American Universities enjoy greater academic and social acceptance than those who have the same level of education from Indian Universities.

When the Indians were first allowed to sit in the ICS examination at London, the success rate in the examination was low, because of the great difficulty in acquiring English education and travelling overseas. Romesh Chandra Dutt, who was one of the first Indians to join the ICS and rose to the position of Commissioner of a Division, found that he had difficulty in following a pro-peasant policy and had to toe the line of his British superiors and resigned to follow an independent path of his own. This is clear from his innumerable writings.[6] Obviously, the British Government wanted people who would serve the cause of the Empire.

After independence, the bureaucratic structure remained the same. The close interaction between the bureaucratic and political system, had the effect of transferring some of the culture of the former to the latter. The political system in an independent democratic country should have evolved a culture of its own instead of adopting the bureaucratic culture. The bureaucratic hierarchical culture is not suited in a democratic system, where egalitarianism must prevail. The colonial system does not believe in equality in fact its very *raison d'etre* is inequality. Along with the colonial baggage, we also inherited the feudal baggage. The society is yet to shake off the feudal shackles and is converting itself from a caste-based one to a class-based one. It has been held by an observer that 'The Indian bureaucracy has social and caste-based elements that place India somewhere between a predatory and a developmental state'.[7]

Lack of Contact and Coordination between different Levels

The rigid bureaucratic structure has resulted in a system, in which there is little or no feedback from the cutting edge staff at the lower level to the higher bureaucracy. It is the lower level staff, who actually services the people and has first hand knowledge of the problems of implementing government programmes. The higher bureaucracy functions either at the policy making level or at the supervisory level. There is no regular consultative machinery in place for interaction between personnel who implement a government project and those who work out the blue prints of the same. There is also often lack of coordination between the supervisory staff and the cutting edge staff. For proper policy implementation, there has to be constant flow of information between different levels of government machinery - both formal and informal.

Mere progress report in statistical form does not always give a true picture of things. Various formats have been devised to obtain progress reports - weekly, monthly and quarterly. But all these reports are only quantitative and the utility of the same is hardly known. Reports and returns, which have been tools of administration over years for routine administration, like criminal and revenue work, have limited utility in the field of development administration, where the quality of work is of utmost importance. It is necessary to evolve a consultative system with field level functionaries for proper implementation of various schemes.

The system of regular inspections of field level offices by higher officials followed by detailed inspection notes, has taken a backseat in the present pattern of administration. This system has not been totally done away with and exists in government manuals, but has lost its importance as an important administrative tool.

One of the main reasons is the neglect of routine administrative work, which is considered by some as synonymous with red tapism and dilatory tactics. Political executives have little patience with routine administration and want quick results, which can be shown as achievements before the next elections. This has resulted in pressure being transmitted down the line and introduction of certain amount of ad-hocism in the system. While excessive dependence on routine at the cost of expediency is not desirable, but certain amount of checks and balances is necessary in public services, particularly while dealing with public funds. This has resulted in removal of many systemic checks in administration, like insistence on routine inspections and proper maintenance of records. With huge public expenditure being entrusted to the administrative machinery, there needs to be enforcement of proper financial discipline. Most of the financial rules are outdated and not designed to handle such huge expenditure.

Financial administration does not form part of general administration and the audit work is mostly post mortem after a considerable time lag. The supervisory officers should be given the specific responsibility of ensuring financial discipline. There is need for rationalisation and modernisation of financial administration. Personnel dealing with schemes having large financial outlay should have knowledge of financial management. In many cases it is seen that officials dealing with large sums of money get into trouble, more due to lack of knowledge in financial matters than any financial delinquency. Supervisory officers at all levels should have thorough knowledge in financial administration, so that they can guide the executing staff properly. The concept of general administration is an outdated legacy of imperial administration. Administrators should have specific knowledge of sectors, they are kept in charge of, without which they will be seriously handicapped in discharging their responsibilities. Frequent transfer of personnel from one post to another is not in the best interests of administration.

In the present situation, with quick turnover of officials, an officer is able to complete a small part of a project, after which, his successor takes over and has to get himself acquainted with matters in his new situation, before he can get down to work. In this process, work gets delayed, with resulting financial loss. A situation, where two or three officers complete a project, nobody can be held responsible for failure of the project. It is like a jigsaw puzzle, where the small portion of the work done by each individual, does not properly fit in, resulting in a distorted work. For failure of the work, everybody generally passes on the buck to his predecessor, resulting in an unseemly exercise in bureaucratic mudslinging. This is the reason, why officers who have retired long since or have been long transferred are at the receiving end of this buck passing, as they are unable to defend themselves due to long passage of time and non-availability of complete records.

Many administrative decisions are dictated by urgency of the situation and any delay may cause serious problems, leading to the loss of life and property. When the dust has settled and the sense of urgency is not there, another person may take a different view as an afterthought. Decisions and consequent actions are taken in circumstances, which sometimes look quite different in the two dimensional world of files and air-conditioned offices, not to talk about various gossip circles and self-styled vigilante bodies. To give a small example, suppose a small irrigation project is necessary to save the crops urgently, the development officer may have to undertake the work immediately, without going through the rigmarole of the time consuming process to the latter.

Unless he executes the project immediately, he will be subject to severe criticism by the public at large and also by his higher authority, besides being branded as an inefficient officer, who is unsympathetic to the people's needs. But by doing this, he is also putting himself in a vulnerable position. At a later date, when an audit is taken up after his transfer, he will be unable to defend himself and the good work done by him will be completely forgotten, particularly with the typical bureaucratic disease of blaming everything on the predecessor. However, if the officer concerned is well connected, or has developed a powerful network to back him, it is very likely that he may avoid any major problem.

Private Sector Model not suited for Public Service

After independence, we have been modelling ourselves to a great extent on the economic and administrative system of the USA. Now, American society does not believe in equality and openly encourages inequality, which is the measuring rod for success. In fact, the concept of success in American society is extreme inequality. The American concept of liberty is pursuit of inequality. American imperialism is a successor to British imperialism. The British economist, Alfred Marshall wrote in the early twentieth century, 'Mass of the people had not realized then and perhaps men do not realize even yet, the grandeur and the moral strength of Adam Smith's large Imperialism, when he proposed that England's Chief Colony (USA) should become the kernel of a great empire, in which she herself should play a leading, but not a dominating part'.[8] We have to be careful in not following the American pattern blindly.

American pattern of management superimposed on the Indian system, with its Guru concept, will tend to create an organisation, where few have monopoly of knowledge. Already there are plethora of management Gurus, whose discourses are akin to religious discourses in corporate circles. The Gurus are supposed to be all knowing and their teachings are to be blindly followed. In the field of natural sciences, the greatest intellect of the last century, Einstein was never considered to be a Guru. The theories propounded by him were not the last word on the subject and were questioned. Management theories, dealing with inter-personnel relationship are unlikely to be perfect and will vary according to circumstances. To put these on a pedestal, will prevent any further innovation. Public administration has been going for management concepts in a big way to set its house in order, by sending its top executives for orientation in management institutions meant for private sector. Private sector consultants are also being invited at huge costs to advise government on restructuring and other vital matters. This is gradually leading to transfer of private sector values to public administration.

Endnotes

1. Plato, *Republic, Book VI,* p.369; Translated by Benjamin Jowett; Published by Walter J. Black, New York, 1942.
2. Karl Popper, *The Open Society and Its Enemies, Volume One: The Spell of Plato,* Routledge & Kegan Paul Ltd., Indian Reprint, 2007. In his notes at page 297, Popper says that Plato's Academy was notorious for breeding tyrants. Many of Plato's illustrious pupils proved to be tyrants as governors/rulers.

   Whether, this was due to Plato's teachings, is open to question. But, the fact remains that the humanitarian idea of freedom and equalitarian justice did not find any place in Plato's theory.
3. Ibid, p.80. Plato's theory of natural inequality is against the very concept of democratic values and is suited for colonial

rule. It has no place in a democracy and poses a threat to a democratic polity.

I can do no better than quote from Herman Finer's monumental work, *The Theory and Practice of Modern Government,* p.952, 1962, Methuen & Co. Ltd. London. "Those with exceptional gifts are not divinely appointed; for all men are divinely appointed or none; they spring from the common body of the people. (I have seen Italian peasants who look the image of Fermi, the great physicist)".

4. Philip Woodruff, *The Men Who Ruled India, Vol. II,* The Guardians, p.76. First published in 1954. Present reference is to Jonathan Cape (London), paperback edition 1963.
5. Ibid, p.76.
6. RC Dutt's two volumes of *Economic History of India* – (i) *Under Early British Rule;* (ii) *In The Victorian Age,* are classics of Indian economic history of the nineteenth century.
7. PB Evans, *Embedded Autonomy: States and Industrial Transfomation* (1995), Princeton, Princeton University Press, referred to in Edward J Malecki, *Technology and Economic Development* (1997), p.292, Longman.
8. Alfred Marshall, *Industry and Trade* (1923), p.734-735), Macmillan and Co. Limited, London.

Chapter - V

Evolution of Administration in British India

British had come to India as rulers. Ruling a country and administering it is different and one should not be confused with the other. Rulers are prima facie in a superior position and can easily enforce their dictat, whereas administration is bereft of the concept of master and servant. Art of administration has to be much more subtle and complicated than the art of ruling. A good administration is basically self administration, which is a corollary of self government. In the words of the great historian Vincent Smith, who had served as an ICS officer, 'The exclusion of Indians (*from public life*) had certain important effects - Public ability ceased to bloom when denied the sun of opportunity'[1] Any art, which is not practised for generations, dies down. It will take considerable time for it to be revived.

As a part of the colonial legacy, the belief persists that whatever damage the British rule might have done to India, this was compensated by providing a stable and efficient administrative system. We were always given a picture that when the British had come to India, they found a lawless country, full of marauders like Thugs and Pindaris, so graphically recorded by William Sleeman in his 'Rambles and Recollections of an Indian Official' and Meadows Taylor in his novel 'Confessions of a Thug'[2]. These reports constitute the basic source materials for the books on Indian history, being taught in our schools and colleges. These accounts are basically personalized ones, in which the author and his colleagues play the central role. As in all memoirs, there will be tendency to magnify one's role and those of his friends to more than life-size. While certainly, these are monumental works and a student of history has to consider the same, while reconstructing the events of that period, they are certainly not the works of impartial historians.

A study of the contemporary accounts of seventeenth and eighteenth centuries will show that brigandage was a common practice in the highways of Europe, including Britain. Although these obnoxious practices had to be put down with a firm hand, they were certainly not Indian innovations in the field of crime and lawlessness. The fact remains that there were no major recorded law and order problems and the villagers by and large enjoyed a peaceful and tranquil existence. If India of the eighteenth century had been a lawless country, it would have been hardly possible to control the same with a handful of people from a distant land. Grotesque and the unnatural attract greater attention than normalcy. But then, if we base our conclusions on such perversities of a few, it would be like missing the wood, for a few rotten trees. Generalisations from a few incidents of criminal perversities do more harm than good.

Picture of India of that time, as a country of grotesque and unnatural, is more a result of cultural shock, arising out of cultural conflict. By all accounts, Indian villages had fairly robust self-governing institutions in the form of Panchayat bodies and were not in need of any foreign administrative intervention in a large-scale, as was envisaged. The British Colonial power wanted to administer India in their economic interest and did so according to their own lights. The economic penetration of the colonial power was down to the lowest level of administration, i.e., the village.

Direct administration of a country as vast as India by a small island nation was a stupendous task and could be possible only because the vast majority of Indians were law abiding. There are no records of any civil disturbances. In such a situation, the problem of administration was comparatively easier. Usually Indians have a tendency to keep their problems to themselves or settle them mutually, without seeking administrative intervention. They expect no favour from the government machinery. It is only a small handful of people, who are favour seekers and frequent government offices. Today the position is different with the wide reach of government and few if any can avoid contact with the government machinery. However, in those days, it can be safely assumed that ordinary Indians had little or no interaction with the government machinery. Probably in the initial stages, the British officers came in contact with those who were only favour seekers and had an axe of their own to grind. It is unlikely that these officials could have any meaningful contact with the Indians, primarily due to the language barrier. Cultural differences also created problems for free interaction. In such a situation some of the perverse practices, given pseudo-religious sanctions attracted greater attention and were generalized.

In the initial stages, most of the Englishmen, who had come to India, were the common riff-raff type and could hardly take an objective view of men and matters in a distant land. When they went back, they painted an exceptionally gory picture of the country. It was depicted to be a country full of oriental despotism and barbarism, sanctified by religion. Such a country needs to be saved from itself and the islanders showed unusual zeal in addressing themselves to the task. Of course, Indians had to pay for the services. The job of administering India provided huge employment opportunities for the youth in Great Britain and consequent economic development. The unemployment problem could be solved in the service of the colonies, paid for by the colonists. This also constituted huge transfer of resources from the colonies.

The Role of Collector

Many of the young men, who had come to India, earlier in the Company's service and later in the service of the Crown, were fired with a missionary zeal, bordering on religiosity to take up the White Man's Burden (a term, so appropriately coined by Rudyard Kipling, much later).[3] They were out to civilize the natives, rid them of their superstitious beliefs and teach them Christian ethics. This mindset continued throughout the British rule. The prime example of this was the Indian Civil Service officer and its manifestation was the role of the Collector of the district. The role of the Collector, originally, a revenue collecting authority, became central to the scheme of things in the administrative machinery of the State, with the powers of the District Magistrate, without which the land revenue collection system could not be effective.

The Collector became the embodiment of the British Crown in the district. Even many of the Viceroys and Governor Generals did not enjoy such powers, being constantly monitored by the Secretary of State, who reported directly to the British Parliament. Many of the Secretaries of State had their own views on the Indian Empire and they were not always in consonance with those of the Governor Generals. Both these functionaries had limited knowledge on India, having never worked in India. Both Clive and Warren Hastings began their career in India as Writers. But after that it became a deliberate policy to send one of the British Nobles as Governor Generals.

Collectors on the other hand were trained to run the Empire. The concept of district administration was a new one, as these matters were earlier left to the local bodies, like Panchayats in India or Borough Councils in England. The management of local affairs was left to the local leadership. This is a system, which for ages has nurtured local leadership. It was never thought feasible or practicable for managing the day to day affairs by a representative of the Crown or Durbar. The British Imperial policy realized early that it was dangerous to allow the development of local leadership. These local bodies may become sources of local power centre and may develop an agenda of local interests, which may not coincide with the Imperial policy, particularly the economic one, which had its ramifications throughout the length and breadth of India.

The office of the Collector was the chosen tool of the Empire to carry forward its policy right from London to the innards of India. This was an administrative innovation of major dimension to implement the chosen policy of the Empire at a time when transport and communication were at the stage of steamship and postal runners. Distance and the long time taken for communication made the Collector free from any control or interference. He was virtually the master of all he surveyed. These enormities of power made a British Civilian say, 'I have played with the harp, whose chords are the hearts of men'. The post of the Collector was a major administrative tool of the Empire.

The Collector was the sentinel of the Empire, the Roman Proconsul.[4] The Empire realized that it was not enough to have the British monarch in London or the Governor General and the Viceroy at Calcutta or even the provincial Governors, it was necessary to have the authority of the Empire closer home. The answer was found in the office of the Collector and the office became more than life-size. It was also realized that merely an authoritarian office will not be good enough; it has also to be seen as a do gooder. A subject nation must have a paternalistic administration and the immediate ruler must give the impression of combining the sternness of the father combined with the tenderness of the mother. Hence the conception of *Mai-Baap* administration emerged, where adult people are treated as children.

This was a heady mixture for any young man and he took to it, just like duck takes to water. The power and prestige of the Empire rested on the shoulders of the Collector and they were taught to believe that they were the guardians, as visualized by Plato in his 'Republic'. 'The men of the service were chosen and trained on Plato's principles as Guardians who would rule in the light of their own vision of the Good.'[5] This vision has to be their own, formulated in a far off country, flushed with imperialistic ambitions and a belief that the Empire was permanent. The British had studied the Indian society and its psyche and realized it would not do to keep control over a country, the size of a continent with a huge population with military power alone and some subtle method has to be found. It was in the office of the Collector that an ideal administrative mechanism of the Empire was found. Their training, apart from academics, was such that they were taught to regard themselves as superior from the natives. 'White man's burden' to civilize the natives is central to the concept of master race.

In the words of a British Civilian, 'The English Guardians certainly believed there was something in their composition that distinguished them from the people they ruled; they were forbidden to own land in India'.[6] The injunction on the rulers for not owning land in India was for the very purpose that they do not develop too close an association with the country and always think of themselves as rulers and keep suitable distance from the local populace. Once a person purchases land and settles down in a country, he will tend to be associated with the local populace and is bound to come under local influence. During the early period of British rule, particularly during the time of Warren

Hastings, there was close interaction of the Europeans with the locals. Even some of them started adopting local customs and as a rule did not look down upon the Indians. Close interaction bred familiarity, which had its own problems, as was amply demonstrated by the celebrated case of Maharaja Nanda Kumar.[7] Here the person concerned was certainly well known to the Governor General, but somehow fell out of favour with him.

The powers at London did not favour a policy of befriending Indians on equal terms and the policy of keeping a reasonable distance from the Indians became the rule. It was of little significance to the rulers that the white man's burden was on the natives, as they had to pay for their masters' upkeep. It was estimated as early as 1844, that the cost of the British administration was as much as Rs. 200 millions. White man's burden was in fact a burden on the Indian people and came at a high cost, which was attributed as one of the causes of increasing poverty in India by the earlier nationalists. Dadabhai Naoroji had raised the issue in the British Parliament even at that time.[8]

Warren Hastings was in favour of a system of indirect rule, with the actual governing being left to the Indians. He wrote in 1772, 'the boys of the service are sovereigns of the country under the unmeaning titles of supervisors, collectors of revenue and administrators of justice'.[9] He understood that the young man's agent was the real master of every supervisorship or collectorate. He wanted the British officers recalled to Calcutta and to collect the revenue and administer justice through Indians. He was also in favour of abolishing the post of district officer, but the East India Company's Board of Governors did not agree to the same, as it would seriously curb their power of patronage. It can now only be a matter of conjecture, how the administrative system in India would have developed had the advice of Hastings been taken to abolish the post of district officer. But one thing is certain that it prevented the development of any local leadership worth the name and made the people, unduly dependent on the administrative machinery. The *Mai-Baap* theory of administration is a corollary to this.

Unlike the British Empire, the Roman Empire was based on a system of indirect rule. Romans introduced the same system of government in their colonies, as in Rome and Italy and involved the locals in the machinery of government, which consisted of bodies like municipal boards.[10] Indian polity would have been quite different, had a system of limited self government been introduced from the early stages of British rule. Instead, the self governing institutions like Panchayati Raj, which had evolved over the ages, were destroyed under a paternalistic system. When the Romans had conquered Britain and Gaul (France), these countries were in a semi-barbarous state and the introduction of their system of self government, prepared the basis of a democratic and civilized form of government. It is a great historical misfortune that Imperial Britain did not return the same favour to India, which they had in their turn received from Imperial Rome, when they were under the same predicament. The major difference between Roman colonisation and British colonisation was that the former was basically confined to Europe, whereas the other was outside Europe, encompassing the entire globe. Roman Empire civilised Europe, without undue exploitation. The same cannot be said of the British Empire.

Warren Hastings's attempt to involve the Indians in the day-to-day administration did not find support from the Company's directors or the British government, in spite of his efforts to convince them that 'the people of India were not savages, that they had laws of their own, that their customs should be respected.'[11] His advice to his namesake, Lord Hastings, when he was appointed Governor General in India in 1817, nearly two decades after he had demitted that office, is worth quoting.

'Among the natives of India, there are men of as strong intellect, as sound integrity, and as honourable feelings as any of this Kingdom... by your example make it the fashion among our countrymen to treat them with courtesy and as participators in the same equal rights of society with themselves'.[12] Noble words indeed! Let us compare this with the views of Cornwallis, his successor, who wrote 'every native of Hindustan, I verily believe is corrupt'.[13] He followed an active policy of excluding all Indians from posts of any responsibility. This became a permanent feature of British administration in India, till at a late stage, they grudgingly conceded a few posts to the Indians.

Roman Empire had a liberal policy and the administration of the conquered areas, was carried out by the local people under an over all control of Rome. It proves that the benevolence of British administration was a lie. The concept that Indians were unfit to manage their own affairs, even at the local level, smacks of a 'master race' syndrome. Vincent Smith, who was himself an ICS officer, observed in his 'The Oxford History of India' that this policy of depriving the Indians of any voice in running their own affairs, had a negative impact on the ability of Indians to carry out public service. Once, a nation is denied the opportunity to govern itself for a century and half, the talent automatically dries up.

Vincent Smith writes 'Public ability ceased to bloom when denied the sun of opportunity. Thus grew the legend that public ability did not and never had existed in India. European and Indian gradually ceased to rub shoulders in public affairs. Personal relations outside the sphere of commerce, tended more and more to be that of master and servant....So developed that contempt for things and persons Indian which was already prevalent in Calcutta in the time of Lord Hastings, and which produced the shallow half-truths of Mill and Macaulay and the downright contempt of lesser men'.[14] This passage sums up the basic philosophy of British administration in India and should be read by a serious student of public administration. Administrative ability comes through practice and tradition. Administration is more an art than a science and evolves with the society. There has to be a symbiotic relation of administration with the society. In India, development of administration has been outside the society by a group of people, who had their own concept of good and bad. It is universally accepted by scholars that good or bad are not universal concepts over time and space. There is a host of literature on the subject. Cornwallis and his ilk should have been acquainted with the works of his compatriot, the Scottish philosopher, David Hume, particularly his 'An Enquiry Concerning the Principles of Morals' (1751).[15]

A nation, as much as a person, who claims universality of his views, suffers from a delusion and has dictatorial designs. This was the basic legacy of British administration, where a people, who had a long developed system of local administration, were made wholly dependent on a distant central administrative machinery. In fact, people were made incapable of administering themselves. This made Winston Churchill, the arch imperialist, say in the British House of Commons, as the leader of the opposition, while discussing the India Independence Bill 'In handing over the Government of India to these so called political classes, we are handing over to men of straw of whom in a few years no trace will remain'.[16] Churchill's speeches and utterances on India are replete with such gems. After the passing of Indian Independence Act in 1947 by the British Parliament, partitioning the country, Churchill sent a message to Mountbatten, the last Viceroy: 'I am very conscious that I put you in to bat on a very sticky wicket to pull the game out of the fire. Few people would have taken it on and few, if any, could have pulled the game round as you have'.[17] Churchill was obviously happy that they were successful in their grand design to break up the country.

There was complete breakdown of administration and law and order in the closing stages of British Raj, brought about by the Government's hands off policy and refusal to bring in the army to aid the civil authorities in the face of large scale violence and complete anarchy. In fact, this was the time, when the first priority of the government machinery, should have been to save human lives. This last episode of complete failure of administrative machinery is a sad commentary on more than a century and a half of administration which claimed the highest standard in perfection. This is a situation where local leadership is called for. In the absence of proper local leadership, there was complete failure of administration and the *Mai-Baap* system could not rescue the same.

Incidentally, the choice of Mountbatten as the first Governor General of independent India was a strange one. As is on record, he had a poor war record and was made the Supreme Allied Commander, South East Asia, towards the closing stages of the war, more as a means of getting him out of direct command from the Navy to a largely ceremonial cum political posts. He was also probably required to keep an eye on the Viceroy, Wavell, who was more sympathetic towards Indians and unlike his successor was less of a politician. Originally, the date of transfer of power was June 1948. But Mountbatten in a cunning move decided to bring the date forward by ten months, when large parts of India were in turmoil due to near civil war situation, leading to complete break down of law and order. He knew that at that point, the bargaining position of the Indian leaders was the weakest and given further time, there is possibility of the situation returning to normalcy. He also posed as the paragon of graciousness by advancing the date of transfer of power, but at the same time pushed through the old British agenda of partitioning the country in haste, with ill-defined borders.

Cyril Radcliffe, the English judge, who knew nothing about India, was deputed to do the border demarcation in a hurry and did a bad job of it, leading to frequent disputes, particularly in the Eastern Sector. There is no doubt that this cunning ploy of Mountbatten led to loss of countless lives and misery in the form of displacement of millions of people. This was the parting kick of British Empire and they extracted a terrible revenge on the Indians. Mountbatten was the chosen agent of this nefarious design and he did the job exceedingly well. Naturally he won plaudits from Winston Churchill, the arch imperialist. He also foisted the Kashmir problem on India by advising the government wrongly. So much as an epilogue on British administration in India.

Cornwallis's irrational belief that Indians are not to be trusted was the basis of the administrative machinery developed by the British Raj. This was a dangerous thing and was designed to condemn the people to perpetual foreign domination. Distrust of the locals was the basis of administration. To support such a system, a network of informers had to be built up. An administrative system must have a system of gathering information. A keen observer of Indian affairs wrote: 'A regime such as that which ruled India depends more upon secret intelligence than does one rooted in popular support'.[18] This was the position, particularly during the last thirty years of British rule, when agitation for India's independence speeded up. However, the fact remains that a system of external administration, which depends upon informers and rumours (or bazaar gossips), can hardly be a rational system and is likely to be paranoid. An open and responsive administration must function in a free and frank atmosphere.

Great Britain did not have an egalitarian society in any of its constituent units - England, Scotland, Ireland

and Wales. It was and still continues to be a highly class conscious society. In this class conscious polity, another lower class - the colonial subjects neatly fitted in. Indians would constitute a lower class than the natives of the United Kingdom. Class or its Indian counterpart caste is a man made social innovation, in which everybody can claim a superior status over somebody. The lowest in the rung in this system is so demoralized that they think that their fate is preordained. Bureaucracy, they devised for India, was based on the same concept. They had also studied the complexity of the Indian caste system and realized that this is a counterpart of their own class system, designed to keep the vast majority in perpetual subjugation. They also understood that Indians are highly colour conscious and a fairer skin carries a natural advantage. In this caste conscious polity, they had no difficulty in occupying the highest position than any Indian. It was only at a later stage that a few Indians were grudgingly admitted to the higher bureaucracy. This was more as a palliative to Indians that a few of them can aspire to reach the level of their masters. It was shown as magnanimity of the British race that they had civilised their subjects to such an extent that a few of them can aspire to reach the level of their masters.

It certainly cannot be said that British administration was an unmitigated evil. They had given an able and impartial administration at a crucial time in Indian history. But their policy of exclusion of Indians from any administrative post, led to the atrophy of this vital art. It would have been certainly a better situation at the time of transfer of power, if they had involved the Indians in administration from the earlier stages of their rule. Administration is an evolutionary art and should develop along with the society.

Social norms and traditions have a great deal of influence on the same. If the society is unable to administer itself for a long period, problems are bound to occur, when the external agency withdraws. An art which has been dormant through generations cannot be revived through the mere induction of a few brilliant people on the system. Strength of an administrative system does not so much depend on the brilliance of a few of its members, but on the strength of the organization. As part of the legacy, suspicion and distrust have been the key elements in our administrative system.

During the Mogul rule, the Delhi Durbar kept control of the huge country by an elaborate system of Subedars and Mansabdars, who owed allegiance to it. Whenever, these potentates became too big for their boots, the Empire had to intervene by sending expeditionary forces to dislodge the pretender. The punishment for any attempt to break away from the suzerainty of Delhi had to be swift and exemplary. Generally the Mogul Emperor dispatched one of his trusted generals as a trouble shooter. The loyalty of the person was generally ensured by his relationship with the Emperor, mostly through a female relation of the former. Besides the family and property of the general leading the expeditionary force could be kept as a hostage.

The control system laid down by Akbar, ensured firm control over the provinces. The Mogul Emperor generally remained in Delhi or its vicinity. It was only when Aurangzeb decided to lead the Deccan campaign against the rising Maratha power and in the process got bogged down in the South that centre got weakened. This effectively marked the beginning of the end of the Mogul Empire, which was hereditary and person based. The Durbar or the power centre rotated round the person of the Emperor. No permanent institutions had been built to sustain the Empire. This was unlike the Roman Empire, where a network of powerful institutions like the Senate and the army existed to sustain the Empire.

The British colonial administration had a precursor in the Roman system, which was the high point of European colonialism and civilization. The European scholars were well versed in Greek and Latin, the languages of the Roman Empire. If they wanted to look up to a model of a successful empire, it had to be the Roman Empire, with which they were well acquainted through various scholarly studies. The Greek civilization was based on city states and they were not burdened with the problem of administering and controlling a huge sprawling Empire. However, the concept of philosopher king, propounded by Plato, was wholeheartedly adopted by the British, particularly in the office of the Collector, although this idea was conceived in the context of a City State, rather than a sprawling sub-continent. They also looked for a secular philosophical base for their system, unlike the Ottoman or the Spanish Empire in America, both of which were religion based.

The Roman Empire was secular and its power was based on robust state institutions like a vigilant Senate, a robust civil administration, a republican army and above all by an alert citizenry. The civil administration consisted of Prefect, with a number of magistrates to look after day to day administration. The judicial system consisted of Tribunes, with the Senate as the highest court of appeal. Even the Roman army during its various conquests did not indulge in plunder and pillage, as the marauding armies are accustomed to. The soldiers were rewarded by grant of land in the conquered provinces to settle down there, after they retired. This acted as a salutary principle that they do not alienate the local populace. Roman law was introduced in the newly acquired provinces. The road network in Europe was built by the Roman army engineers. This network still serves as the road system in Europe for motorized traffic.

Although the Britons had learnt the lesson of imperialism from the Romans, the basic difference was

Britain's search for empire was to bolster her nascent industrial revolution. This required colonies for economic exploitation. Moreover, the Roman Empire being mostly European based had no racial problem and assimilated the people of the conquered provinces. They did not have to bear the imaginary cross of the white man's burden. Britain's policy in acquiring its Indian Empire was not for settling its surplus population in an already overcrowded country, but as a colony for economic exploitation. However, they realized that unless a country is properly governed, it will not be possible to develop it as a subsidiary economy. Britain wanted a stable country with a peaceful population, to have a colonial partnership, certainly not on equal terms, but as a supporting economy. India was ideal in their scheme of things. The efficient administration that resulted from the British rule in India was a product of that policy.

Plato's vision of the State was a totalitarian one and suited an imperial system of government with the concept of master and servant. Whatever may be the merits of this system of appointing a young man with very definite idea of good and bad, it will certainly not help in developing any local leadership, which is fundamental in any democratic system. The system of pre consul is a throw back on the Roman Empire and is devised as an extension of the power of the Roman Caesar, situated at Rome. The British Imperial system found this administrative tool of the Roman Empire, very useful indeed in maintaining its authority and presence in far flung areas of the Empire, when modern system of transport and communication was not in existence.

It is a matter of conjecture, what India would have been had the Britons not taken over control of India, at that point of time, when there was a decline in the authority of the State. They had come to India at a time of the decline of the Mughal Empire (proverbial Delhi

Durbar). This led to local chieftains ascertaining their authority, without checks and balances. Britain realized, it would not do to have merely a strong central power in Calcutta (original British capital of India) or even in the provincial headquarters and there is need for the presence of British power through the length and breadth of India to have a lasting Empire. The office of the Collector proved ideal for this purpose, with its *Mai-Baap* (mother and father) syndrome.

This was an ideal administrative innovation, in which the district official was the embodiment of the sternness of the father and the tenderness of the mother. This concept is ideally suited for a paternalistic society, where the individual has no existence outside the family and the father exercises supreme, almost divine power. The father's dictat cannot be questioned and is sanctioned by the scriptures. He has the good of his children (even if the children have become adults long since) at heart and can do no wrong. The mother is the embodiment of tenderness and is always there to wipe away tears from the eyes of her children, even if the father has become excessively demanding. Of course the father can never overstep his limits and the children are duty bound to carry out his wishes and not to question the same. This father-mother fixation is typical of the Indian male and continues till a late age. Even after the demise of the parents, god men of different hues take their place. This concept of non questioning submission to an earthly authority is typical of the Indian psyche. Such characteristic is common in a settled agricultural community and not in a community of hunters or nomads, where much more individual initiative and independent decision making capacity is required, for the very of survival.

This concept is extended from the family to the state. A fatherly state provides comfort and security to people and there is need for something more tangible to represent the state. District was a convenient administrative unit and its administrative head would ideally fill the bill of a paternalistic figure. The idea of a benevolent administration was admirably suited for India with a settled agrarian population, not given to much adventure, with a taboo on crossing the seas. The success of the post of Collector as administrative machinery was not so much due to the power conferred on the functionary, but due to the prestige attached to the post.

The Collector was not merely the head of district administration; he was the eyes and ears of the government. In fact, he was the embodiment of the government in the district. The Collector was, however, never vested with such power that the functionary can become a tyrant, even one with noble intentions. The power of the District Magistrate as regards administration of justice was merely a ceremonial one, with separate judicial machinery. In non-regulated areas, District Magistrates also had judicial powers. But this was mostly a temporary measure and an exception, rather than rule. Criminal Procedure Code, till it was amended in 1973, gave power of taking cognizance to executive magistrate, before committing a case for trial by a judicial magistrate. Investigation of a case was purely a police job, with very little control by the executive magistrate. Criminal Procedure Code of 1898 did not contain any provision allowing the executive magistrate to interfere in the investigation of a case by the police. This has been the view of the Privy Council "the court's functions begin when a charge is preferred before it, and not until then".[19] Similarly, the Collector had very little control over other departments functioning in the district, which had their own departmental heads.

The position and authority of the Collector rests on the fact that he is considered to be the representative of the government. During the Colonial administration, he was 'our man' in the district. As such he enjoyed considerable autonomy and could take independent decisions, as being the man on the spot. In the olden days, when transport and communications had not developed, the Collector was a powerful presence in the district. He could take independent decisions, as the circumstances demanded, even when specific government approval was not there. His superiors seldom questioned his decisions, as they were from the same fraternity. One does not hear of a powerful Commissioner, but there are many instances of successful and effective Collector.

It was well realized that an Empire can be won by arms, but to maintain the same, a standing army will not do, particularly in a country of the size of a continent and with the imperial power at a great distance. There is need of suitable administrative machinery to sustain the Empire. A good and effective administration was necessary and the post of the Collector admirably filled the bill. An impression was created in the minds of the people that the Collector was there to protect them from rapacious revenue officials. The memoirs of the officials reveal that they had nothing but contempt for the subordinate field and clerical staff and were of the opinion that their very presence prevented anarchy in administration. It was only the presence of a benign district head in the guise of an Englishman, which kept the rapacious native staff from exploiting the common folk. This was of course a myth sought to be built up, but the strangest thing was that, all concerned came to believe in it.

The post of Collector became more than life-size and evolved into an institution by itself. As with everything in human affairs, myths play greater role than reality and rationality and this myth came to stay. To maintain an Empire, administration was of paramount importance and it was inconceivable to imagine a district without a Collector. The incumbents assured of full support rose to the occasion on the belief that they were discharging the white man's burden in the service of God and Empire. Empire became a matter of faith, entrusted by the Almighty on the British nation and its maintenance became a sacred duty.

The members of the All India Services were appointed by the Secretary of State in the British Cabinet and owed allegiance to the Whitehall and not to the Viceroy in India. This is significant, in that the All India Services were directly responsible to the Secretary of State for India in the British Cabinet. This gave them full operational power and prestige in India. It was a deliberate policy to have a set of officials in India, who are directly appointed by the British Crown and are not unduly hampered by interference from any functionary there. It is of interest to note that till 1920, bulk of the ICS consisted of Europeans. This can be seen from the figures indicating the strength and composition of the ICS from 1859 to 1939, given below: [20]

Year	Europeans	Indians	Total
1859	846	-	846
1869	882	1	883
1879	907	7	914
1889	884	12	896
1899	988	33	1021
1909	1082	60	1142
1919	1177	78	1255
1929	881	241	1122
1939	759	540	1299

The British came to seriously believe that the ideal of the philosopher king of Plato had been achieved in the person of the District Officer (Collector). 'The English would be remembered, not by this institution or that, but by the ideal they left behind of what a district officer should be'. (Lord Wavell said in an informal speech, long after he left India).[21] This ideal institution came into conflict with the elected representatives, immediately after the same came into place under the Government of India Act, 1921. The Royal Commission on The Superior Civil Service in India was constituted in 1924, under the Chairmanship of Lord Hamilton, with equal number of European and Indian members.

Commission in its report stated that the constitutional reforms brought about with Ministerial responsibility, backed by a legislature, have led to deterioration in relationship between the political classes and the Services. Ministers in the provincial governments particularly resented the fact that All India Service officers, who were working in the provinces, were continued to be appointed by the Secretary of State in London. The problem of duality of control of services emerged when elected governments were formed in the provinces in accordance with Government of India Acts. In fact, there was steady deterioration of law and order during the last phase of British rule, which the administration failed to contend with. Bengal famine of 1943 was a classic case of complete administrative failure, for which nobody took any responsibility.

Endnotes

1. Vincent Smith, *The Oxford History of India,* Fourth Edition edited by Percival Spear (1981), p.532.
2. An admixture of cult murders and bizarre religious superstitions has made the story of Thugs, a fodder for

popular romantic novels and horror stories and films. In fact these types of things are the grist of the mill for pot boilers. Acts of highway brigandage have been given the image of a religious cult, in which Hindus and Muslims were equally involved, although their religious practices of both the denominations differ. This point itself raises the question of credibility of the existence of such a cult. Moreover, if the cult (with its basis in pseudo religious practices) was so widespread, it could not have been eradicated by a single civilian officer (William Sleeman) of intermediate level (Sleeman was Superintendent and later promoted Commissioner of Thugee and Dacoity Department), with a handful of poorly trained sepoys within a span of ten years. It is as if the Thugs were waiting to be eradicated by Sleeman. Thugs were certainly no religious zealots, but common criminals and brigands, with no strong organisational base. One thing is certain that Thugee was not based on superstition, but on criminality. The problem of highway brigandage, has been oversimplified. Had it been a major and chronic menace, based on strong religious overtones, it could not have been eradicated so easily.

The net result has been that the name of Sleeman has become synonymous with 'suppression of Thugee'. It catapulted him to the notice of the Governor General, Lord William Bentinck (1828-35), who was particularly interested in ridding the country of abhorrent superstitious practices. Sleeman's one man exploits and reports earned him a Knighthood and the rank of Major General. Another interesting aspect is that in most of his exploits, he did not have a British Assistant, who could have given a corroborative report. The entire story of Thugee is based on the uncorroborated version of a single person, who came out as a great Saviour. This is, however, a common bureaucratic practice and is quite prevalent even today.

3. 'The White Man's Burden' is a verse written in 1899 by Rudyard Kipling on his return from India and published in the same year. It is available in Internet Modern History Source Book. This is not an isolated piece of writing, as some apologists for Imperialism, have tried to make out. Kipling's books and verses, particularly 'Kim', are

replete with the role of White Man in civilising and administering colonies.

Kipling's perception was the commonly held belief of the supremacy of White Races over the colonial subjects, put in an imaginative and catchy perspective. Those interested in sociological imperialism can refer to Edward W Said (2003), Orientalism, Penguin Books and Culture and Imperialism by the same author, published in 1994 by Vintage Books.

The concept and tool of imperial administration was administering a lower order of people. Such a system of administration is not suited for an independent democratic country. Our carrying on with the same pattern of administration has naturally created problems.

4. Roman Proconsuls were in charge of the provinces of the Roman Empire and had full magisterial powers. They were the representatives of the emperor.
5. Philip Woodruff, *The Men Who Ruled India,* Vol.II, The Guardians, Jonathan Cape (1963), p.15.
6. Ibid, p.76.
7. Maharaja Nandakumar (also called Nuncoomar) was a Mughal Indian tax official, who succeeded Warren Hastings as Collector of Burdwan in 1764. As happens in officialdom even today, he developed a long standing rivalry against Hastings.

   When Hastings became the Governor General and had a running war with his Council, some of its members, particularly, Philip Francis, used Nandakumar as a cat's paw against him. In this running battle, Nandakumar came out the worst. He was tried on a charge of forgery, committed earlier, convicted and hanged. The trial and conviction were according to the English law of that time. The message sent out from London was clear that Indians should not meddle in the affairs of the Europeans.
8. Dadabhai Naoroji, while addressing the British House of Commons as a Member on August 14th, 1894 had said on the British administration 'the main features in the last century were gross corruption and oppression by the Europeans; in the present century; high salaries and the

heavy weight of the European services'. Then again 'What advantage had been derived by India during the past 100 years under the administration of the most highly-praised and most highly-paid officials in the world? If there was any condemnation of the existing system, it was in the result that the country was poorer than any country in the world.' He has also quoted several British Ministers and Statesmen to support his views. (Dadabhai Naoroji, *Poverty and Un-British Rule in India,* 1901, pp.264-65 & iv-x). Obviously, this was not the opportune time to publish the self adulatory memoirs of John Beames, which will have to wait for another sixty years. This will be further discussed in note 12.

9. Philip Woodruff, *The Men Who Ruled India,* Vol.I, The Founders, p.128.
10. Edward Gibbon, *The Decline and Fall of the Roman Empire,* Vol.I, p.41-43, Everyman's Library.
11. Philip Woodruff, *The Men Who Ruled India,* Vol.I, p.124.
12. Ibid, p.124.
13. Cornwallis's views (Vincent Smith, *The Oxford History of India,* p.532) of distrust of Indians seem to be the mindset of the British officers from that time onwards. The distinction became sharp between rulers and ruled. This is the refrain of the British officers, as is seen from any of their memoirs. They can at best be patronising to the Indians, but never treat them as equals.

    To cite a typical instance, John Beames, who according to some represented the best face of British colonialism in Orissa and served as Collector, Balasore (1869-1873) and Cuttack (1875-1878), had very low opinion of the subordinate Indian staff of the Collectorate. (John Beames, *Memoirs of a Bengal Civilian,* Chatto and Windus, London, 1961). He positioned himself as a saviour of the common folk against a corrupt and rapacious lower order Indian officialdom. Beames also considered his junior Indian colleagues inferior to their British counterpart. His deposition before the Aitchison Committee at the time of Ilbert Bill controversy shows him as an unapologetic racist. This is perhaps the Hyde side of his personality. But there is a Jekyll side to it too. (RL Stevenson, Dr Jekyll and Mr Hyde)

Beames made a signal contribution to the preservation and development of Oriya language and culture and was held in high esteem in Orissa. He was also the champion of the underdog, according to his own lights. When the Salt Law was being blindly enforced against a poor person, he intervened and pointed the inequity of the law to the Government. As Collector, Champaran in Bihar, he intervened in favour of a peasant cultivator, when the latter complained to him about harassment by a British Indigo Planter. According to his own accounts, he did this more to spite the Planter, to show who the boss was. Was it benevolence or clash of egos?

He was the typical British district officer, who did not brook treating any Indian as equal, at the same time condescending to the poor. Self proclaimed one person army (which has only a General and no soldiers), fighting an imaginary battle for the poor, with a monopoly of righteousness and virtue. This was the recipe for success for a colonial administrator - a combination of Christian ethics and colonial power and arrogance. It is highly unlikely that a District Collector, with a complete distrust of his subordinate staff could achieve any tangible result. But, in human affairs, generally form is more important than substance.

Our present purpose is to study the legacy of British district officer on the present administrative system. Even today our model of a good administrator is the British Collector of yore. This nostalgia for British Collector, has been created by a plethora of Raj books, giving a more than life-size image of the functionaries. It is perhaps no accident that the Memoirs of John Beames was decided to be published nearly hundred years after it was written. After passage of so many years, it is difficult to say how much of it fact and how much fiction. It is certainly not desirable in a democratic system to take such officials, with their arrogance and self righteousness as role models to be followed.

While lamenting on the performance of the present day administration, there is some amount of nostalgia, that if we could have administrators of the ICS calibre, administration would have been much better. Attempts are made to replicate the ICS standard by rigorous training in the same methodology and deputing the front runners to foreign universities. Foreign universities are always considered better than Indian ones. However, it has not been possible to replicate the ICS officer, the simple reason being the gulf between myth and actuality. The picture of a super administrator is based on self extolling memoirs, rather than reality. Moreover ICS officers are products of colonial administration. This should not be considered as any attempt to belittle their individual brilliance or integrity. But to hold them as model administrator in today's situation will send wrong signal to aspiring administrators. The role of an administrator in a federal democracy will have to be completely different.

14. Vincent Smith, *The Oxford History of India,* p.532-33.
15. David Hume, An Enquiry Concerning the Principles of Morals (1751). Hume was one of the founders of the Scottish Enlightenment and precursor of the Open Society concept, which is of fundamental importance in a democratic system. His quote 'Where men are the most sure and arrogant, they are commonly the most mistaken', is an eloquent indicator of his philosophy. BBC recently voted him the Greatest Philosopher. Unfortunately, the philosophy of David Hume was not in the course of study in the training schools of civil servants.
16. Quoted from Hansard in *Liberty or Death* (1997), Patrick French, Harper Collins Publishers, p.308
17. *Liberty or Death,* Patrick French, p.309.
18. Ibid, p.99.
19. AIR 1945 PC 18 in the case of King Emperor vs. Khwaja Nazir Ahmad.
20. *The Men Who Ruled India,* Vol.II, p.363.
21. Quoted in ibid, p.360.

Chapter - VI

Collector in Post Independent India

We have seen that the role of Collector was central to the British administrative system. This post continues to be in the same position in post-independence India. The Central Government wanted to have its representative in the state administrative machinery and the concept of All India Service admirably suited the scheme of things. The post of Collector, which was the exclusive preserve of the Indian Administrative Service, remains the most visible part of the administrative machinery. This post symbolizes the federal system of government, with a unitary bias. The postings of these functionaries are entirely at the discretion of the state government and the Central government has no say in the matter. The Collector and the Superintendent of Police being the two most powerful posts at the district level, the state government attaches the utmost importance to these postings. Generally this is the prerogative of the Chief Minister and he guards it very zealously.

The Collector of a district is basically the nominee of the Chief Minister and in practice he holds the post at his pleasure. Generally the practice in the government machinery is to phone up the Collector, in case any information is wanted immediately. Sometimes this may be of general importance, but many times the matter relates to a particular case, which is quite of a routine nature and need not take undue precedence at the cost of other problems, which may be of equal or greater importance. Collector is generally considered to be our man in the district and is as such required to be also the ready reckoner for the district.

It is many times not recognized that it is physically not possible for the Collector to have all the detailed information about everything at any given time and that he will have to get back to the concerned officer, before giving a correct report. Insistence on immediate reports, even on matters of administrative details, results in wrong information being given and subsequent cover up operation. In fact over dependence on the Collector on all matters, creates a problem of its own. As too much is expected of the Collector, transfers from these posts are frequent, for failure to meet the expectations of powers that be.

The Collector has to function within the framework of the rule of law, but the expectation from him is much more, for which rules have to be bent. This is a danger zone in administration, as there is sometimes little difference between bending rules and breaking them. It has been seen on a number of occasions, a dynamic and energetic Collector getting into trouble, when a close scrutiny of his work is made by a successor government or by an agency which has different perception of the matter. This is also possible, when the successor has a different view of things and has also powerful backers. New incumbent sometimes starts with a well publicised view that nothing much was done earlier and he is trying his best to set matters in order. This type of thing is not uncommon, particularly when each Collector has to set his priority from the numerous tasks entrusted to him. It will be quite impossible for a Collector to give all the plethora of jobs equal importance and he will have to pick and choose. A particular official may have given greater importance to health projects in the district than other development projects or vice versa. This makes him vulnerable from the champions of supposedly neglected sectors and if they are powerful or influential enough, the official may find himself in difficulty.

The office of Collector is unique to the Indian sub-continent. While the British Colonial administration introduced this system for their Indian dependency, they did not have a similar system for their own country, where city councils and borough councils were the basis of the administrative system. The post of Collector was basically conceived for a unitary system of administration, to execute the policies of the Central Government. During the period of transfer of power from the British Raj to the independent Government of India, the Indian polity was in turmoil, due to the trauma of partition and development of other fissiparous tendencies in different parts of the country. The national leaders of that time rightly decided to continue with the existing administrative system. It was thought at that time, that the office of the Collector, being manned by an officer from the Indian Administrative Service will have an All India outlook and act as a unifying force in the administration of the country. All India Service in administration and particularly the post of Collector was the administrative machinery available for pushing the Central Government schemes through the length and breadth of the country. This became necessary with the Central Government assuming complete control of economic development of the country through the plan process.

Collector as Prime Mover in Planned Development

The post of Collector is of vital importance to the Central Government's scheme of things, as this office is used for pursuing its policies, especially those affecting the general public. The First Five-Year Plan (1951-56), which ushered in planned growth, clearly mentions in the plan document that the post of the Collector has been central to the Indian administrative system for more than a century and should continue as such. In fact the role of Collector, which was so far primarily confined to law and order and land revenue collection, was expanded further to make it central to the plan process. The Collector became the chief development officer in the district and in that capacity was in supervisory charge of virtually all other departments in the district. He was also put in charge of ensuring people's cooperation and participation by acting as the chief extension officer. Guiding local self governing bodies and ensuring that they discharge their duties fairly and in accordance with law, also constitutes one of the duties of this office.

The power envisaged for the Collector is enormous indeed. But this is not followed by giving the Collector necessary legal backing, opening the way for administrative wrangles with other departmental heads in the district. The result of all this is that the Collector gets bogged down in endless coordination meetings to the detriment of his normal executive work. Moreover all the government agencies working in the district are line agencies, being controlled by their respective heads of departments; many of them are experts in their own line, with considerable experience. In such a scenario, the Collector will have to do lot of tight rope walking to keep a balance. In any case, this provides a fertile ground for clash of egos and administrative conflict, once the Collector becomes over enthusiastic in a specific matter, which falls within the jurisdiction of another department.

The Indian five year plans were conceived on the model of Soviet five year plans drawn up by Gosplan (State Planning Board). But unlike the Soviet Union, there was no machinery in place for implementing the Central Government schemes. In the Soviet Union, Communist Party functionaries were in charge of implementing and supervising the schemes. This led to limited success. As is now known, the success of the Soviet plans was highly exaggerated through state propaganda machinery and the foreign visitors were taken on guided tours, so that they get an impression of economic miracles. Leaders, especially from countries, which have been recently liberated from foreign yoke, replicated the Soviet model of planning in their own countries. India was one of the first countries to go for the Soviet model of planning; even the duration of the plan period was the same as the Soviet plan of five years and the Planning Commission at the Centre taking the role of Soviet Gosplan.

Soviet plan ran into trouble, right from the beginning. There was opposition from the peasantry to the rapid industrialisation drive, which had been envisaged in the plan process. Even the Communist Party of the Soviet Union was divided on the issue. This led to the great purges of the thirties, when most of the top leadership of the Communist Party of the Soviet Union was liquidated. The middle and lower leadership got the hint and fell in line. However, the limited success of the Soviet plan was due to the fact that party machinery was put in action, with a cadre of party functionaries, known as apparatchiks, to implement the central directives. It worked successfully under the iron leadership of Stalin. But once Stalin left the stage, this system deteriorated fast, with the party functionaries cornering majority of the benefits. This led to a new class of Red Czars, which came to light for the first time in a book clandestinely written by Milovan Djilas, titled 'New Class' (1957).[1] Eventually, the corruption and mismanagement by party apparatchiks reached such a proportion, that it led to the collapse of the economy and break up of the Soviet Union. Worse has been the fate of Yugoslavia, a model of liberal communism. In the Soviet Union, due to mismanagement by party functionaries, shortages of essential commodities and failure of the public distribution mechanism led to complete economic chaos. The failure was not that of the ideology of Communism, but of the execution machinery.

India, being a multi-party democracy, did not have a cadre of party officials to implement the policies of the Central Government and so had to depend on All India cadre of officials for execution of their programmes. The motivation of these officials to be in line with the thinking of the Central Government was essential for successful implementation of the policies of the latter; hence, the great emphasis on training for motivation. In fact, the entire training given to a new recruit to the IAS is structured for functioning as a district officer. The long drawn training schedule, which a new recruit has to go through, is meant to prepare him for his eventual posting as Collector.

The Indian Administrative Service is closely associated with the post of Collector in public perception and hence a long training period for an assignment, which is likely to be for about an year for most of the persons. There is little or no training for Secretariat procedure and practice, although all IAS officers are required to spend the major part of their career in the Secretariat. There is also no training for public enterprise, which is one of the vital instruments for planned economic development. There is also no training for financial or personnel management. The variety of jobs required to be handled by an IAS officer, will require an exceptionally long training period, which is quite impracticable. While there has been emphasis from time to time on horse riding as an essential ingredient of IAS training, an important but lowly art of type-writing has never been included in the curriculum. In fact knowledge of this important art of secretariat procedure would have made the officers self reliant and not always dependent on their stenographers and private secretaries. This could have prevented leakage of classified information to undesirable elements, creating serious problems. However, the picture of Collector on horse back was too ingrained in one's imagination.

Horse-riding is associated in the Indian mind with feudalism and colonialism. It would be considered infra dig for an officer to be seen typing an urgent and important document. In administration as in other spheres of life, form is more important than substance. There has been, however, no reported instance in recent times of any Collector going on inspection tour in his district on horse-back. This may be to some extent due to the stoppage of allowance for maintenance of horse after independence, as the government did not want to display their representative to the people as a throwback on colonialism and feudalism. While the government policy in the matter was clear and they did not want any melodramatics on the part of their officers, the training institutes run by bureaucrats had different ideas.

The political executive was happy to leave the training of bureaucrats by bureaucrats, as it did not affect their constituencies. But when it came to actual working, they had different ideas from the rigmarole of long bureaucratic training. In fact it was necessary to unlearn many things of the training to function effectively and not be seen as tilting at windmills in a quixotic fashion. Ideas of the trainers may not suit the actual conditions. Even if the trainer was an expert, his expertise may have developed under different conditions and his prescription may not apply under another set of circumstances. A long and costly training programme does not necessarily equip a person to face the rigours of the job better. In fact it may give him some wrong ideas which may get him into difficulties, unless he quickly debriefs himself. The idea trying to be ingrained in young officer-trainees to ride a high moral horse, as if he has the monopoly of virtue may be very counter productive. The officers have to work with the system. If to his mind certain things are not what it should be, he should try to correct it without trying to strain the system.

Training system of the future higher officers, which we have inherited from our erstwhile colonial masters, is basically based on the theoretical concept of Plato's philosopher king. This concept never took any practical shape in the Greek polity. It was resurrected after centuries by the British for their colonial empire, particularly India.

Training of philosopher king envisaged by Plato is politically motivated to create a class of rulers. 'This has remained a major function of higher education down to our own time'.[2] In training institutions for new recruits, unlike universities, there is a tendency to moralise and impose one's ideas of good and evil. At least, this was the situation, I found during my time in the National Academy of Administration, where the Director had very clear cut ideas of good and bad and attempted to impose his philosophy on the trainees. He wanted to build up the trainees in his own image. Such a method is not at all suited for a democratic system. If one takes this training too seriously, he will be looked at as quixotic and will get into trouble. Fortunately, nobody takes these things too seriously. But then it is a huge waste of time and resources.

The training designed is a generalised pedagogic one and should be kept at the minimum to prevent undue drain on the public exchequer. The cost is twofold. The undue long period spent by the young recruits on training at an age, when they are at the peak of their ability and energy and can spend their time in more productive work like the job for which they were recruited, is certainly a huge wastage of manpower, which a poor country can ill afford. Since the training is at public cost and the trainees are drawing their full salary, there is added burden on the exchequer. Moreover the probationary officers have already completed a long academic career and will be looking forward to doing some responsible job and not be cooped up in a training institution, which is only an extension of college or university.

An undue long training period has the effect of demoralising an active young person, who is raring to get on the job, for which he had applied. A long period spent as a student, when he is dependent on the society in place of his parents, is unlikely to do much good for a person's self confidence or self esteem. Training was essential for a foreign recruit to administration as he was going to a completely new place and people, of whom he knew next to nothing. Moreover he had to be trained in the concept of Empire. As the cost of the training was borne by the colonial country, it did not affect the British exchequer.

The policy of planning and implementation of our developmental plans is formulated by the Central Government. This obviously cannot take into account the problems of local variations and conflict with local interests and power groups. These groups have local support and no development work can be taken up without their active cooperation. A Collector or a government official does not function in a social vacuum and he has to work with the people, which means the interest groups. In some cases, interests of these groups and local interests may not always coincide with Central Government policies. For example, the policy of suddenly closing down factories, which are not able to maintain national or international health or environmental standards, is likely to create local opposition, which may snowball into a major agitation. In such cases, it is necessary to assess the impact on the local economy and populace of such a decision and take remedial measures. Similarly acquisition of agricultural land in a hurry for industrial or other purposes, without studying the implications on the local economy have been creating major problems. These are problems of major socio-economic dimensions and the policies cannot simply be pushed forward by the official machinery, with the Collector at the spearhead. There can be numerous instances, where local situations require a different prescription than an all pervasive national or state policy.

The effectiveness of an officer posted as Collector depends on his knowledge of the district and its socio-economic conditions; particularly, since in administering various economic development programmes in the district his role is also one of a major socio-economic administrator. Putting a person suddenly as the district administrator and expecting him to provide quick fire solutions, is unlikely to be very useful. It is necessary that an official posted as Collector, has experience of working in that district earlier in any of the posts like, Sub Collector, Additional District Magistrate, Project Officer or in any such post. This being generally not the case, it is necessary that a person posted as such, gets himself acquainted with the conditions in the district.

Earlier, there was a system of Note to the Successor, in which the previous incumbent is to leave a detailed note for his successor, outlining the latest position regarding different schemes, as well as his assessment of the general situation in the district. This was an important document, meticulously written and designed to brief the new incumbent. This document was also intended to maintain the continuity of administration. This practice has long gone into disuse, as the new incumbent has a different brief and wants to chart a path of his own, unencumbered by the views of his predecessor. The practice of sudden transfers, gives little time for a person to pack his baggage, let alone write an elaborate note to the successor. Sometimes, a Collector is asked to leave the district within twenty four hours or less. The message being that he is a bad bargain. This is highly demoralising for the person concerned, but worse is that it demeans the office in public esteem. Effectiveness of a government office depends on the public estimation of the same and not simply on the power conferred. It demoralises the bureaucracy and holds it up for ridicule in the public eye. The result is irreparable damage to a vital institution of administration, particularly since the Collector is required to be the point man of the government in all important matters in the district.

Earlier there was even a system in which the old Collector was asked to stay on for a few days to informally brief the new incumbent. This practice has been discarded long since. There being little scope for such informality these days. Mostly, Collectors are given little time to settle down to his work or leave his post in an orderly and dignified fashion. Suddenness of the transfer is construed as a shock therapy for the administration. In fact, the result is generally the opposite, putting the administrative machinery in disarray. Frequent shock therapies are no good for any disease and certainly not the best way for administrative reforms.

Bureaucratic transfers, particularly at the state level are ad hoc in nature and this is more so in the case of Collectors. These transfers do not follow any set of principles or guidelines and is purely based on the discretion of the government, which is in fact a euphemism for whim. In view of this, officers are always at tenterhooks, as to when the thunderbolt of transfer will hit them. Needless to say, this is hardly conducive for good and efficient administration. An officer may have just settled down to his work, when he is faced with a transfer order, making a nullity of much of the work he has done, as some influential element is not happy with him. Higher officials have to be experts in public relations to keep all concerned happy. This is certainly not the best thing for administration. An official, who goes all out to project himself and continues to look at himself in the mirror of publicity, will have little time or inclination for anything else.

Frequent transfers and postings have created an unsure bureaucracy, where nobody is sure of his position. The message, which is being sought to be transmitted, is that the Big Brother is watching you. This is very much an Orwellian situation.[3] Incidence of transfers and postings is highest in the Indian Administrative Service, the premier service in the country. Average tenure of a number of officers works out to one year or less. An officer may be working as the Managing Director of a corporation dealing with Information Technology; he may suddenly find himself in a supervisory job dealing with preparation of land records or welfare of Scheduled Tribes.

This exercise of transfer and posting cannot certainly be conducive to administrative efficiency. This is contrary to the concept of a permanent bureaucracy. Max Weber in his classical definition of bureaucracy emphasized two features: security of tenure and monopoly of expertise. Security of tenure does not mean security of government service. It means fixed tenure in a particular job, which can only develop proper expertise. Unless a person works in a post for a reasonable amount of time, he is unlikely to develop expertise on the job. Thus the classical concept of bureaucracy, which is accepted throughout the world, is not applicable to the Indian higher bureaucracy.

Security of tenure in a job for an official is of vital importance, as the political executive does not enjoy a fixed tenure, due to the election process. Frequent turnover from one job to another reduces the efficacy of the bureaucracy. Quick changes in the Ministerial berths in the British Cabinet, led George Bernard Shaw to make the scoffing remark in the preface to his 'The Apple Cart' that 'the nearest thing to a puppet in our political system is a cabinet minister at the head of a great public office'.[4] While this was certainly an exaggeration and we know that there were statesmen of eminence, heading various cabinet portfolios; frequent transfers do not improve the public image of any organisation.

In the present pattern of administrative system in India, turn over in higher bureaucracy, is much faster than that of political executives. This is particularly true of most of the states, where much of the work of running the administration in India takes place. In fact, the administration of most of the central programmes is the responsibility of the state governments. Post hopping has eroded the public image of bureaucracy and has diminished its operational efficiency. Mercifully, we do not have a Bernard Shaw here!

Unscheduled and frequent transfers are regular features in the administration of most of the state governments. IAS officers are particularly vulnerable to this disease. This is probably in the nature of the Service itself. IAS officers are appointed as head of organisations, where they are not familiar, either with the work or personnel, working therein. The idea being that higher management does not require detailed working knowledge of the organisation or its personnel. This is a managerial concept, particular to the IAS and its *raison d'être*.

From the inception of their service career, it is drilled into the minds of young IAS officers that they should be prepared to serve in any job anywhere. Whereas 'anywhere' is not much of a problem, as most of the postings are in the state headquarters, the problem relates to 'any job'. Probably, they were believers in the Jacksonian view that the duties of public office are so simple that they can be entrusted to almost anyone with intelligence. IAS officers, having cleared a tough all India competition, are certainly intelligent, but expecting them to deliver results, in a system of musical chairs of transfer and postings of one year or less, is not realistic. Jacksonian view emanates from President Andrew Jackson, the seventh President of the United States, who introduced the spoils system in government jobs. In his opening message to the US Congress in 1829, he said: 'The duties of all public officers are, or at least admit of being made, so plain and simple that men of intelligence may readily qualify themselves for their performance'.[5] This simplistic view of the public offices certainly does not hold good after nearly two hundred years, when public administration requires professional administrators with fixed tenure and responsibilities.

When we joined the service in the mid sixties, IAS cadre was in the formative stage in the State (Orissa), to which I was assigned. Direct recruits were at a fairly junior level. Bulk of the officers at the senior level were emergency recruits, with back dated seniority and with limited years of service left. There were also officers from the state service or service with the ex-Princely states, who were promoted to the IAS. The group was therefore a heterogeneous one.

There was also, an imbalance in the cadre, with officers from outside the state more in number than the locals. The state government was keen to make up the shortfall of local candidates in the direct recruitment quota. When more number of local candidates started qualifying for the IAS from sixties onwards, the state government increased the quota of intake of IAS officers.

However, they had to abide by the 'All India Service Rules' of equal representation, that for every local candidate allotted, another candidate from outside the state has to be inducted. This situation continued for the better part of the sixties. Then suddenly, they thought that they had enough and more or less stopped the recruitment for a few years. After a few years of this, it was business as usual and recruitment again picked up from the mid seventies. This type of sporadic recruitment policies are hardly the best way of cadre management. It creates glut of officers at particular levels, creating problems in adjustment of officers in posts commensurate with their seniority and experience. This creates demoralisation amongst the officers and creates a feeling of being unwanted, which is hardly a pleasant feeling.

In our time, when one joined the state government for further training, on completion of training at the National Academy of Administration, it was customary to call on the senior officers during the Secretariat phase of the training. When we would call on a particular officer, he would invariably enquire about the number of people in our batch. On being told that there were eight of us in the batch allotted to the state, as was the case with previous three batches, he would pass some snide remarks, as to why so many officers are being allotted to the state. He would also wonder aloud, how so many of us are going to get duty posts and it would be difficult for the Government to find even sub-divisional postings for us, not to mention later postings as District Magistrates and beyond. He would not also, fail to mention that in his time only two or three persons were allotted to the state. Some would also not fail to mention that with such huge intake of new recruits, quality of officers was bound to suffer. It was conveniently forgotten that over the years educational opportunities had also increased and the competition had become keener with a greater number of candidates appearing for the competitive examination. However, the warning was not, altogether misplaced. Some of us did have difficulties in getting proper postings during our service career. The message was also quite clear that unless, we have or manage to cultivate powerful connections with people, who matter, the future is unlikely to be too bright. Careers in the civil service are undoubtedly built on powerful connections, either inherent or acquired.

At this stage something needs to be said about the policy regarding the number of direct recruits being inducted to the IAS each year. The service is under dual control of Central and state governments. The former routinely asks for an annual indent of requirement of new IAS officers to the states. After this the Personnel Department (earlier it used to be the Home Ministry) calculates its overall requirement, keeping a margin for Central deputation and leave reserve posts. After this exercise, projected requirement goes up. The Centre is the final authority for deciding the total requirement of officers and states are only recommending bodies. Once the officers are recruited, they are allotted to the various states, which are their cadre controlling authority and have the responsibility of fitting them in suitable posts during their service career. Centre takes no responsibility in this matter. There is also no post in the Government of India for an IAS officer, unless the State deputes him. This dual control often creates mismatch between the actual requirement of the states and placement by Centre. As has been the experience in almost all cases in the past, dual control is never a satisfactory arrangement. Even before independence, there were problems regarding diarchy in administration and particularly in the higher civil service.

Policy of recruitment also depends on the policies regarding development needs, particularly rural development. It was realised that elected bodies will not be able to deliver results without proper administrative support. Moreover, feudal or vested interests may dominate the elected bodies and the benefits of development may be cornered by the better off sections, leaving the poorer sections high and dry. It was thought that a dedicated cadre of bright young persons should be sent out to the countryside to carry through the policies of the government. At one stage, in the early sixties, it was thought that young IAS officers would function as Block Development Officers and subsequently as Secretaries of Zila Parishads (Elected District Development Bodies). This would require considerable expansion of the IAS cadre and accordingly recruitment was increased. However, this experiment was given a good bye to, as disenchantment with the existing community Development arrangement had already set in.

Move Towards Panchayati Raj

Community Development and National Extension Service were designed for rural development, with the inception of economic planning from 1951. Various evaluation reports of the government found that the projects were benefiting only the better of sections, who were elected to the Panchayat bodies. The need was felt for greater official intervention, so that there was more equitable distribution of benefits, which were being generated. The existing official arrangements at the block level were not found very satisfactory.

United Nations Technical Assistance Mission came to India in 1960, at the request of the Government of India, to evaluate the results of the Community Development in India. Amongst other things, they found that there was little or no communication between villagers on the one hand and the officials and the elected office bearers on the other. They found 'the patience and capacity for listening to villagers which was brilliantly demonstrated by some of the top level officials was found wanting in officials in lower rank'. There was a language barrier between the officials of the mission and the lower level officials, who were not accustomed to English conversation those days. It is generally village touts who come to such meetings and will be overjoyed and get an ego boost in snubbing the lower level functionaries before their superiors. Particularly, since the former interact with the latter on a day to day basis and who might not have been able to accede to many of their undue requests.

The top officials will be too happy to score favourable points with the UN representatives at the cost of their subordinates, may be with an eye at a UN berth. This is a typical bureaucratic disease, of superior officers trying to humiliate subordinates and scoring points at their cost. It may be an ego booster, but it demoralises the subordinate officers, who have to carry on with their work, once the dust of these flying visits have settled down. These temporary visits by foreign experts serve little purpose. If we are not able to set our house in order, it is unlikely that foreigners will be able to do so. In any case, these types of stage managed things during flying visits need not be taken too seriously. However, since they emanated from the UN personnel, who were foreigners, they were taken seriously and formed the basis of personnel policy for heading the development blocks.

The very concept that foreign or top officials, who do not work or live amongst the villagers, will be more sympathetic to them than the lower level officials, who work and live amongst them, is a throwback on the colonial pattern of administration. We have to remember that the colonial administration was based on the precept that Indians are not capable of administering themselves. Top officials trying to get a pat on the back from foreign visitors, is not very healthy for our national prestige.

Ideas imported from outside do not always suit the local conditions and their sudden introduction creates more problem than they solve. To cite an instance, in the earlier stages of community development, emphasis was given on improving the sanitary habits of the villagers. Mahatma Gandhi had spent considerable time on educating the villagers on this elementary, but important matter. Gandhian method was slow and results can be expected gradually. But nobody had time for such long drawn methods and we wanted instant modernization. With this idea, there was a project for construction of Western type flush toilets for villagers, who were living in thatched houses. The project was an utter failure and resulted in waste of public funds. Villagers, who did not have basic amenities, had no use for this device. On the other hand, the attempt through education and persuasion and local innovation through practical and cheaper ways yielded better results. Barpali Panchayat Samiti in Western Orissa did a pioneering job in this aspect, which was a model for rural sanitation in the entire country.

In fact the key to rural development lies in local innovations and channelizing local energy and not in mindlessly spending money on grandiose schemes. The latter is much easier and quicker, but gives little tangible benefit to the villagers, whereas, the former method, though slow and more laborious, gives better results. The concept of planning from below, which had been recommended in the early stages of planning, has been *bid adieu* long since. In the globalised age, such a concept is considered an anachronism.

Community Development blocks were started with the concept of democratic decentralisation and development of local leadership. It was thought that entrusting the local leadership was the best way to achieve development of the villages. In 1958, Government of India approved the recommendation of the Balwantrai Mehta Committee regarding democratic decentralization and the outcome was elected bodies at block and district levels, known as Panchayat Samities and Zila Parishads respectively. Next few years were the honeymoon period with democratic decentralization. But problems soon came up. Denied of any experience in local self government over long years of foreign rule and accustomed to a paternalistic administrative system of the *Mai-Baap* type, local leadership could not come up to the expectations of the planners.

Community Development system had already short circuited technical line agencies like Public Works Department. In view of this quality of work was invariably poor, due to lack of proper technical guidance and financial laxity. The idea was that Panchayat bodies will be able to execute smaller projects like water harvesting structures, irrigation tanks, village roads to improve the connectivity and irrigation facilities. They were also required to take up construction of projects, which would directly benefit the village community and do not require much technical or administrative supervision. A junior engineering personnel, Engineering Overseer (subsequently designated Sub Assistant Engineer), attached to the development block was thought to be adequate to take care of the minor technical details. Chairman of the Panchayat Samiti as the administrative head of the block had full administrative power, with the block development officer, as the executing authority.

Execution of engineering works without proper technical supervision, invariably led to poor quality of work. Projects were also hastily conceived, more on local pressures than on technical viability. There was also no provision for regular maintenance of the project, after its completion. It was assumed that the village community would maintain the same through its voluntary contribution of labour. Now, nowhere in the world, a village community is a harmonious entity, but a collection of individuals or groups, whose economic interests vary. Moreover, through years of foreign rule, community leadership had become moribund and over dependant on the administrative machinery to take up the responsibility of maintenance of any public work. In view of this, these works were not maintained and had a very short life span. The picture of an ideal village community, which would be the engine of development with a little momentum provided by the government machinery, on which the community development projects were based, was too simplistic to be practical.

When serious doubts regarding the administrative and financial capabilities of the local leadership surfaced, the planners fell back on the administrative machinery. Seventies saw new innovations in the field of development agencies, in which the role of the administration was pivotal. Since the district is the basic unit of administration, Collector became the key functionary in developmental matters. *Garibi Hatao* agenda of the seventies led to special schemes for small farmers and agricultural labourers. Development programmes like Small Farmers' Development Agency, Marginal Farmers' Development Agency, Agricultural Labourers' Agency and Tribal Development Agency, amongst others came into existence. In all these schemes, Collector was invariably the Chairman, with an administrative officer as Project Director. Greater and greater responsibilities were placed on the District Officer on matters, which should normally be handled by elected local bodies for greater involvement of local people. Without proper cooperation of the local populace, implementation of any scheme is likely to face difficulties. Involvement of elected local representatives has to be an important component of any development process. Panchayat experiment, which has been revived, is a step in the right direction.

Musical Chairs of Transfers and Postings

The new recruits with a long innings before them have hardly any career guidance and are not sure what type of jobs they will be required to handle. Transfers and postings are dependant on official vagaries. The guiding principle being that IAS officers should be prepared to serve in any post and be prepared for transfer without any notice. The entire thing was designed to develop a footloose cadre of officials without professionalism of any kind, who would be looking over their shoulders for their next transfer. If anybody dared to question this, he was sternly silenced or given some platitudes. In this situation, it was hardly possible to develop any professionalism.

I recollect, in the early seventies, when I was Deputy Secretary in the state government, Agriculture Census was started for the first time and I was dealing with the subject. It required some technical expertise and knowledge of economics. As I was a student of economics and had some knowledge of statistics, I examined the matter thoroughly and sent a detailed note to the departmental Secretary, who had little time for such elaborate notes and probably could not trust me with a technical matter and referred the file to the Director, Bureau of Statistics & Economics for his views. A meeting was called for. The eternal bureaucratic solution to all problems! In the meeting, the Director initiated the discussion and expressed his appreciation for my note which had provided the basic theoretical groundwork for the scheme. This was not appreciated by the senior administrative officer, who advised me to confine myself to administrative matters and not to bother about technical matters, which were the domain of technical officers. So much for any attempt at professionalisation! It is difficult to construe as to what constitutes administrative matter and what non-administrative matter.

Working satisfactorily in any job requires some amount of on the job training, which is not available to most of the IAS officers. There are of course, lucky exceptions. However, there is no system in place, in which an officer of that service works in an intermediary level and subsequently takes over charge of an organisation. An IAS officer suddenly finds himself to be head of a corporation or a department, of which he had no previous experience and asked to deliver results immediately, which the previous incumbents supposedly failed to do. This is certainly a tall order and no IAS officer has a magic wand. The officer spends some time in getting acquainted with the organisation. In the meantime, his superiors are becoming increasingly impatient for results. When the high expectations of turning round the organisation are not met, the person is transferred and another posted in his place. This is the case with majority of officers and government institutions. There are of course some lucky individuals who enjoy longer tenure and are rewarded with prized posts. The basic idea seems to be that the secret of good administration lies with a few selected individuals than the systemic strength of the organisation. Administrative system believes more on individual efficiency than organisatonal efficiency. For ensuring administrative efficiency, it is necessary to build up a strong organisational structure from within by creating several tiers of leadership, both formal and informal.

In any field of activity, particularly in administration, it is hardly possible to keep every one pleased, when the interests of different individuals or groups clash. Administrative officers, also act in a quasi-judicial capacity have to hand out decisions, which will obviously be not to the liking of one party. For example in a case dealing with land reforms (which in fact means restructuring the land tenure system in favour of cultivators), suppose the decision goes against the prescribed ceiling surplus land holder (ex-landlord), it will earn the official powerful enemy, as such persons are generally highly influential. On the other hand, if the decision goes against the cultivators, he will be labelled anti-poor. There are numerous such cases under different laws, which are being dealt with by officers on a daily basis. Judicious decisions are not the best way to popularity for the executive, particularly when there is no educated and conscious supporting bar, as in the case of judiciary.

The Collector, generally being new to the district will have to spend considerable time in getting acquainted with the place and the people to be effective. Theoretical training cannot be a substitute for practical knowledge. Adhocism in the postings of Collectors should be avoided, if proper results are expected from this functionary. Collector's post has to be a tenure post of three years or more. At present the average tenure of a Collector is generally about an year or less. This is fair neither to the people of the district nor the person concerned. An official posted to a district, has to spend the first six months in getting to know the problems of the district and its people. After that he has to have a plan of action for implementing various programmes in the district. Unless, a well thought plan is worked out at the district level, there will be problems and bottlenecks at the implementation level. Thus, it will take an official about an year to put his plan of action to work, unless he chooses to work in a mechanical fashion.

With so much of expectations on the Collector, he must have a vision for his district and not merely be an administrative cog, biding his time for greener pastures. In addition to his usual task of maintenance of law and order and revenue collection, the Collector has been entrusted with development work in the district, since the beginning of the plan process, making him the chief development officer. Besides, he has also been entrusted with overseeing various social reforms measures. He is also the chief social reforms officer in the district, entrusted with the job of protecting the interest of the underprivileged. In fact, the tasks entrusted to the Collector are daunting indeed! With these onerous tasks reposed on this official, it is necessary that the post is made a tenurial one.

The tenure should be a fixed one, with a period of three years. Any longer period is not desirable, as the official concerned may consider himself indispensable for the post and various lobbies and vested interests may develop round him, without his being very consciously aware of the same. It is also not desirable that in a democratic set up, a non elected official should assume complete leadership of the district. This will certainly cut across local leadership. With an all powerful Collector, local leadership will languish and will not have an opportunity to develop. If local leadership is not allowed to develop through democratic channels, it may grow in undesirable directions like Naxalism or even worse, like mafia type organizations. Official machinery cannot be a substitute for local leadership.

Although posting of the Collector is done by the state government, but the official, being a member of the All India Services and being appointed by the Central Government, is also under its remote control. This assumes, particular importance, as the officers from the All India Services look forward to postings under the Government of India, where the opportunities for career advancement are much greater than in the states. In fact, almost all the important posts in the Central Government are filled up by the IAS officers. In such a scenario, the officers are keen to be posted with the Government of India, quite early in their career, preferably after completing a posting as Collector. They are therefore keen to make a good impression on the functionaries of the

Central Government, when they visit a district to review the implementation of Central programmes. As the finances of the country are under the control of the Government of India, almost all the schemes are financed by them. As they generally finance the major part of the project, their functionaries have the right of review and inspection. The periodic inspections by these officials are of considerable importance, as a favourable report from them is essential for continuous flow of funds. This does not create much of a problem, when the governments in the Centre and state belong to the same party, as the state leadership is under the control of the party high command at the centre. The problem occurs, when the state leadership and the central leadership belong to different parties.

Reviews and inspections by the Central Government officials are post 1970 phenomena. Earlier, Centre used to be content with laying down policy guidelines and leave the execution to the state governments. Frequent interventions by officials may strain the relations between Centre and state. Particularly, when there is a tendency among officialdom to treat the state government officials as junior partners. A strong Chief Minister may resent inspections by the officials of the Government of India on the constitutional principle of federalism. The Government of West Bengal on many occasions has not allowed any Central intervention, without authorisation from the state. It must be said to the maturity of our political leadership that the problems have not been allowed to snowball and have been sorted out. These vital matters of Centre-state relationship should be dealt with at the political level and not at the official level. Good Centre-state relationship is the very corner stone of the federal structure of our democratic system to maintain the unity and integrity of India.

The state government keeps a close watch on the work of the Collector, as their performance and reputation depend to a great extent on the latter. The system of fortnightly confidential report has come down from pre-independence time and still continues. In this document, the Collector is to report, all important happenings in his district, during the preceding fortnight. However, greater emphasis is placed on informal contacts and he is expected to pass on information on important developments without any loss of time. Collectors in sensitive districts or districts considered important by the Chief Minister have direct access to him.

The performance of the government is judged by the execution of the various government projects in the districts and how various sections of people are reacting to the same. In fact, the fate of party in power depends to a great extent, on its record in the district, during its incumbency in the government. As the Collector is expected to oversee almost all the work in his district and keep himself briefed about important matters in the district, he becomes more than an administrative functionary and assumes a quasi political role. An effective Collector is supposed to market the policies of the government. Chief Minister, at the helm of both administrative and political machinery, considers the Collectors as his chosen and key official in both these functions and demands their full loyalty. To keep himself posted of the happenings in the State, pro-active Chief Ministers, do not generally depend only on official reports, which come through official channels and are delayed and diluted in the process and like to have direct contact with the Collectors. This cuts across various intermediary official channels.

Nowadays, with the availability of computers, computer-savvy Chief Ministers have made it a point to be abreast of the latest developments in the state and also issue instructions through video conferencing with the Collectors. This cuts across a plethora of intermediary official channels between the Collector and the Chief Minister, making the official hierarchical system redundant. Most of the Chief Ministers will feel constrained, if they have to depend on layers and layers of bureaucracy, which have proliferated over the years. It will take considerable time for a report from the District official to reach the Chief Minister through the Secretariat channel, as it would be examined at different levels, before it reaches him. The report will obviously be outdated by the time, he can officially look at it. In the meantime, the situation might have changed considerably, making the report all but useless for all practical purpose. Hardly any Chief Minister will condescend to this practice and has tried to get out of the system by organizing his own secretariat, without dismantling the existing system. The official power centre has shifted from the official Secretariat to the Chief Minister's Secretariat in the state, in line with the Prime Minister's Office in the Centre. This has also led to increase in bureaucracy.

As has been discussed above, the District Collector is central to the administrative scheme of things and enjoys certain degree of independence in the performance of his duties, as being the man on the spot. The basic idea seems to be that it is easier to deal with a single official and make him responsible for the functioning of the government in the district, than deal with an amorphous official group, where nobody can be held accountable, as each functionary has only a part responsibility. All these make the Collector, a powerful official indeed, which is rare in a bureaucratic scenario. At no stage of his career, an IAS official enjoys such power and prominence, as while functioning as Collector. In fact, the whole *raison d'être* for the IAS would seem to be for the post of District Officer. This is an anomalous situation, as the post of Collector comes very early in the career of most of the IAS officers, sometimes hardly within five years of service. In any case, one will seldom find any officer in the district, with more than ten years of service. The post is basically meant for a young person at an early stage of the career and an unusually long training period is geared to that end. It is more of the youthful dynamism than seniority and experience. In a society, where authority is generally based on seniority and experience, the post of Collector is an exception, but in view of the long colonial tradition of this post, the incumbent does not face much difficulty. Collector is to administer the policies laid down by the government, but due to the fact that he is to take on the spot decision, he has considerable discretion of his own, within the ambit of government policies. No other bureaucratic post enjoys such power.

After exercising such powers and enjoying so much prominence, the officer has to reconcile himself to playing a second fiddle for the rest of his official career. This transition is generally difficult. However, if, one has powerful patrons, either through cultivation or relationship, one can look forward to greener pastures. With politicians depending more and more on the bureaucrats for their effective functioning, a resourceful officer, can aspire for powerful posts, with perks. Since, we do not have the system of vetting by the Legislature like in the USA, even for the Constitutional posts, the executive is supreme regarding deployment of personnel.

Endnotes

1. Milovan Djilas, *The New Class – An Analysis of The Communist System* (1957). Djilas was one of the architects of establishing the communist government in Yugoslavia and rose to the rank of Vice President. He was disillusioned with the system, which led to his writing this book from his personal knowledge. The book was originally published in the West from a smuggled manuscript.

2. Karl Popper, *The Open Society and its Enemies* (2007), Routledge Classics, in two volumes. Contains a thorough exposition of open society Vol. I, p.157.
3. George Orwell, *Nineteen Eighty-four,* is a profound anti-Utopian Novel that examines the dangers of totalitarian rule.
4. George Bernard Shaw, *Prefaces by Bernard Shaw* (1934), p.323, Constable and Company Ltd., London.
5. Felix A. Nigro, *Modern Public Administration* (1970), p.249, Harper International Edition.

Chapter - VII

Towards Committed Bureaucracy

Climb through the bureaucratic hierarchy is a long and strenuous one and ambitious bureaucrats have little patience with such a time consuming process, which puts them in sight of power towards the fag end of their career. Since power lies with the political executive, it is the proximity with them, which is the source of power and such proximity can generally be achieved through the post of private secretary or secretary to the potentate (Chief Minister or Minister). Since the incumbent for the post is a personal choice of the Minister, administrative formalities like seniority or evaluation of character role, have generally little to do with such postings. This provides an avenue for ambitious bureaucrats to exercise enormous powers, which will not be possible in the usual bureaucratic system. With the political executive being busy in various political activities, which are a priority for him, as a public representative, he has limited time to get into the details of administration and has to depend on a person, who enjoys his complete trust. As such great deal of power on matters of administrative details rests with this functionary, without any formal delegation.

Politicisation of Bureaucracy

The problem of bureaucratic hierarchy has been solved to a great extent by creating a separate regular Secretariat for the Chief Minister, in line with the Prime Minister's Office in the Centre. This is more a bureaucratic innovation and is designed to link up the bureaucratic system with the political one. Since, both the general Secretariat and the Chief Minister's Secretariat are headed by IAS officials, both are integrated in the bureaucratic milieu. The term 'Committed Bureaucracy' has become redundant, as the political and administrative systems are now fully integrated at the Executive level. Secretary to the Chief Minister, who is invariably from the IAS cadre, is a powerful bureaucrat and wields considerable authority by virtue of his proximity to the Chief Minister. This post is in the borderland of politics and administration and wields considerable clout. The post is outside the purview of normal secretariat system and has no statutory responsibility or duty, but has become extremely powerful and important over the years. The bureaucrats must be on good terms with him. Even in many cases ministers of the government take pains to cultivate him for his close proximity to the Chief Minister. Where the person concerned has been able to win the confidence of the Chief Minister; he virtually becomes his alter ego.

The Chief Minister, who is a political person and concerned with his political fortune, is happy to leave many administrative details, to his Secretary. Having a free access to the Chief Minister, he advises him on placement of personnel in key places and virtually works as his eyes and ears, particularly in the bureaucracy. In many cases, he acts as an informal sounding board for the Chief Minister in formulating important decisions. This has led to a considerable extent to the politicisation of bureaucracy. Nowadays, such posts have proliferated both in the state government and the Central Government and have provided avenues for ambitious bureaucrats. The appointment to the post is not guided by the official criteria of seniority and other official paraphernalia and is purely a personal choice of the Chief Minister or minister.

MO Mathai, who was the Special Assistant to Jawaharlal Nehru, first Prime Minister of independent India, nearly from the beginning of the latter's tenure as such, was referred to as 'the most powerful acolyte of the PM' by CD Deshmukh. He had to resign, when the opposition raised several issues against him, including his American connections. Although he was cleared of any financial misdemeanour, the PM had to admit in a press conference, clarifying the matter on the wake of his resignation, 'My broad appreciation of Mr Mathai was of efficiency, integrity and loyalty, at any rate loyalty to me; but also a person who acted foolishly often in small matters; and sometimes rather threw his weight about'. As Nehru has rightly mentioned, the criterion is of personal loyalty. But in a democratic system, the criterion of loyalty should be to the institution, rather than to a person, however exalted his position may be. Nehru was too much of a democrat not to understand that these posts breed a cult of personal allegiance, which may not be synonymous with systemic loyalty. The oath of allegiance is to the Constitution only and not to any person. This is not to imply that the persons holding these posts have been lacking in organizational loyalty. But the fact remains that the primary requirement for this post is personal loyalty.

The necessity of these posts arises because the political executives do not want to get constrained by the normal bureaucratic procedure. They feel that they can deliver their briefs better, if they are free from the procedural details, which constitute the checks and balances of any administrative system. After having won a mandate from the electorate, the elected political executive wants to implement the political agenda, which has brought him to the fore. He has little patience with the paraphernalia of bureaucratic checks and balances. This brings him in immediate conflict with the existing administrative system. Manning the posts of Personal Secretaries by officers from the All India Services is aimed at integrating the Personal Secretariat with the General Secretariat. This has the effect of cutting through the Rules of Business. This also creates two power centres in the government system - one the general Secretariat and the other the personal Secretariat.

Gradually these posts have become ingrained in the system, although there is no constitutional provision for the same. Mathai's autobiography, 'Reminiscences of the Nehru Age', casts some light on the functioning of this important office, although in the process, he has crafted a larger than life picture of himself. This is quite common in these types of autobiography by ex-officials. However, bereft of these, the book provides some vital information. According to his account, he had no problem with the top bureaucracy, which was the ICS bureaucracy. NR Pillai, then Cabinet Secretary sent the character roles of all the ICS officers to Mathai and wanted him to read these voluminous reports so that he can advise the PM on top bureaucracy. If it was so, it was hardly the right thing to do. Bureaucracy had no difficulty in accepting this arrangement in their scheme of things. The problem occurred with the members of Parliament and ministers, who seem to have resented his undue importance and took to referring him variously as 'Deputy PM,' 'Power behind the throne'.

The reaction about this post was a mixed one in the beginning. While the top bureaucracy did not have much reservation about this post, ministers and legislators did not take too kindly to this arrangement. In fact, there was resentment in some quarters, as is seen from the deliberations in Parliament in the Mathai case.

Dominant Rule of Parallel Bureaucracy

Nowadays, such posts have been fully integrated in the bureaucratic system, with a full-fledged secretariat for the Prime Minister and Chief Ministers of states. Almost all the important functionaries have a large number of staff attached to them, constituting a mini secretariat. The available official machinery in the form of a regular secretariat system, where every functionary has an independent role, is obviously not adequate for proper discharge of the duties of higher functionaries. Thus there has grown up a parallel bureaucracy, in addition to the existing bureaucracy. The role of this bureaucracy, is extremely important in the decision making process of the government. This has also led to centralisation of power. The Prime Minister's Secretariat and the Chief Minister's Secretariat are headed by career bureaucrats, who know the rules of the game and will hardly create the faux passé, as happened in the case of Mathai, who came into conflict with important members of Parliament. The bureaucratic content of these Secretariats have also led to integration of these institutions into the administrative system. The integration has been so perfect, that nowadays these are accepted as part of the system and no questions are asked about them, although they exercise considerable amount of power.

These posts assumed importance during the seventies, with the concept of committed bureaucracy. This concept enunciated by the then Prime Minister Indira Gandhi, had a far reaching effect at the bureaucratic level. Ambitious bureaucrats started aligning themselves, either overtly or covertly with powerful politicians. The term 'committed bureaucracy' has been variously interpreted. When Madam Gandhi was asked to clarify, as to what she meant by this, she said she meant commitment to public good and to the policies of the government. The bureaucracy, however, took the hint that henceforth mere adherence to rules will not do and they will have to be more proactive. Merely citing rules for inaction will not be good enough; they will have to find a way out of the legal tangle. I cite a typical incident on reliable evidence.

During the early seventies, the finance minister of a particular state had come on a visit to his constituency. As he was an important minister in the Cabinet, in addition to the local officials, heads of departments from the state headquarters, were in attendance. There were complaints from some influential local people that a culvert on a particular stretch of the road was not being constructed, in place of the existing vented causeway, in spite of their demands. As these people were political supporters of the minister, he was extremely annoyed at such official callousness on the part of officials. Now, as it happens, there were cultivable lands on both sides of the road and a culvert at that particular point was not technically feasible and would have prevented proper drainage of water, leading to water logging in the field of some of the farmers, who were not present in the meeting. This would have also damaged the road system, not being in accordance with sound engineering principles. The Chief Engineer pointed out to that any structural change at that point will not be in accordance with the existing rules. The minister wanted to see the relevant rules. When the rule book was placed before him, he just tore off the page containing the rule and asked 'now show me the rules'. This happened in Punjab. But the same thing would have happened in a different form in any other state, with a less vigorous culture. In most of the places, the matter would not have been so dramatic, but the officers concerned would have been punished, mostly through transfers to less important posts.

The system of committed bureaucracy was just beginning. In this case, the Chief Engineer had taken the responsibility, but this seldom happens and the blame is generally passed on to a junior functionary. This type of thing hardly happens these days. Both the parties have found a way out of this impasse. The local officials generally take care of the local power brokers and vociferous elements, who would normally prefer to be in the right side of local administration, to get their work done and work as sort of intermediary between government agencies and the general populace. A sort of symbiotic relation has developed between both the parties over the years. It is of interest to note that the executive officers exercise quasi-judicial powers amidst a plethora of rules and regulations in a society, which has become more and more complex. There is no system of lawyers, unlike the judiciary to help them in the process and a system of unofficial intermediaries has developed over the years to fill this vacuum.

In tolerance in Bureaucracy

The disease of intolerance of others point of view is also not uncommon in the bureaucracy and has been increasing over the years. In the early seventies, a Chief Engineer had a difference with the Chief Secretary over certain issues. He wanted staff, according to the yardstick prescribed in the Works' Code, since large amount of funds had been placed with the department. He pointed out that release of funds without adequate supporting staff would lead to lower quality of work and wastage of public funds. Earlier Chief Engineer, who was a good public relations man, never pointed out any such problem and tailored reports about progress of work were being sent, showing good progress of work. All concerned were happy.

The new incumbent was releasing funds according to the capacity of the working divisions. This did not please many of his subordinate officers, who were used to a more relaxed system under his predecessor. Some of them had contacts at the highest level and reported surreptitiously that the new Chief Engineer was delaying work. The contractors were also not happy, as they would prefer placement of more funds with less of supervision. They also had powerful lobbies of their own, reaching the very top. The authorities in the state government were becoming restive, as funds from the Central Government could not be spent, as per their schedule. The funds were placed by the Government of India, although the state government did not have adequate infrastructure to handle such large influx of funds. When funds are offered by the Central Government, no state government will venture to ask for a certain concession of time on the ground of strengthening the implementation machinery.

There is intense lobbying for Central funds amongst the states and any slight delay would have led to diversion of funds to another state, creating furore in the State Assembly and the local press. States, which can spend the funds allotted by the Centre quickly, are rated efficient and further funds are placed at their disposal. The criterion of efficiency for officers is according to their capacity for spending funds. Those who lag behind in this rat race for expenditure are considered laggards and dealt with severely. This intense competition to spend public funds creates a phony situation and is one of the root causes of large scale corruption in public expenditure. The projects, which are to be executed at the ground level, are to be surveyed, planned properly and have to be technically sound. A detailed procedure has been prescribed for this in different government manuals and codes. With everybody in a hurry, rules laid down in the code become a casualty, opening the flood gates of corruption.

Intransigence of the Chief Engineer was not taken kindly by the government. The Chief Secretary called a meeting of the heads of departments to review the progress of work. The Chief Engineer, being wary of a public humiliation, sent his Superintending Engineer, dealing with the subject to represent him in the meeting. Chief Secretary and the Works Secretary took serious exception to this and the Chief Engineer was summoned post haste to the meeting. The Chief Engineer was asked by the Chief Secretary to explain the short fall in expenditure from the target fixed by the government department, to which he had the temerity to say that he had kept the latter informed of the shortage of staff and the need to create extra posts, according to the existing staff yardstick in the Works Code and that he had no magic to deliver results. This was quite new to the authorities; accustomed to acquiescing subordinates and the Chief Secretary tauntingly asked him, whether he will have magic in case additional staff is made available. The Chief Engineer said that there will be no need of magic, if he is given the required staff. That was the end of the meeting. But that was not the end of the episode.

In a few days time, some old unproven allegation against the Chief Engineer was dug out and he was compulsorily retired from service. The system of compulsory retirement had been just introduced in the service rules and proved a handy tool to discipline inconvenient senior officers. In this case the Chief Engineer did not have his rule book torn, for the audacity of quoting the same, but was just shown the door. Much less of dramatics were involved, but the message was clear. 'Question Government instructions at your peril'. A new era of intolerance in bureaucracy had emerged. Senior officers were being publicly humiliated for failure to toe the government line unquestioningly. Once the senior officers are demoralised, they will be hardly in any position to give any protection to their subordinates and stand up for them. They will be equally intolerant with their subordinates. The result is a demoralised bureaucracy. There is no need of any political interference. Bureaucracy can very well adept itself to the wishes of its master.

Role Reversal

Bureaucracy is a highly hierarchy conscious system and one must know his place and should not speak out of turn. These days, the methods have become more sophisticated and subtle. Some junior officers, who are close to the power centre, are given the job of floating a new proposal for quick implementation. This may be done in a meeting or in the form of a note. The proposal may look innocuous, but has broader implications, which need to be discussed and thoroughly examined. In fact, the entire paraphernalia of the secretariat system is meant for examining the viability of different schemes and their financial implications. There must be budget provision for the proposal. This latter is a constitutional requirement, as budget grant for any scheme has to be voted by the legislature. Overall financial control lies with the legislature and not executive. The legislature, however, has little time for detailed financial scrutiny of all the schemes and much of the financial power is with the executive. There are frequent cases of diversion of funds from one project to another and to an altogether new project.

Once the powers that be, want to implement something, there is no question of any lengthy notes of discussion or any differing view point in any meeting. Bureaucracy has adapted itself to the situation admirably. Earlier, these matters used to be discussed in file and all concerned used to give their views in the matter. This had the advantage of discussing the pros and cons of the proposed scheme and the capacity of the government machinery in implementing the same. The practice was a healthy one and was a check on half-baked schemes, which run into rough weather soon after their launch. It also had the element of accountability. Policy formulation has ceased to be the job of regular secretariat. Policies mostly emanate from above and have to be only communicated.

Role of Outside Agencies

Over the years, international agencies have been having greater and greater role in policy matters. For example sharp devaluation of the rupee and the virtual abandonment of the socialistic policies from the nineties were forced on us by the IMF and the World Bank. It was a matter of TINA (there is no alternative). The policies of global financial Czars have deprived our government, the power to effectively control the financial market, particularly the flow of foreign funds in the economic system. This has led to a run away inflation, which is attributed to global financial forces and is beyond the control of government. Similarly foreign aid bodies like DFID have a lot of say in the policies of sectors of government, which they are funding. While funding public sector reforms in states, they had effective control of restructuring the public sector units, by recommending the closure of many units. Now, these units were set up in public interest and summarily closing those down may not be the best policy. The conclusion seems to be that we are not able to manage our own affairs and have to depend on foreign bodies to bail us out. Similarly in the field of health administration, the obsession of these bodies with the problem of AIDS in third world countries, have led to the neglect of rural health services, while failing to make much headway in AIDS control, for which no workable scheme has been put in place.

Dilution of Responsibility

Days of rule bound bureaucracy were over and the ambitious bureaucrats assumed a proactive role. This led to the politicization of bureaucracy and the line between politics and administration got blurred. Administrative innovations were resorted to and decisions were made more and more through Committees of Secretaries to the government. This was quicker in the sense that it cut through the red tape of interdepartmental consultations, as envisaged in the rules of business. It also diluted the responsibility, as no single individual can be held liable. There is obviously safety in group action. While this is possible in the Secretariat, the field level officials do not enjoy this luxury. Collector has to function in splendid isolation and is squarely responsible for all decisions, he has to take. Similar is the position of other field level functionaries.

The system of control over field level functionaries has weakened considerably, as detailed regular inspections have become notional. Previous system of regular inspections and follow up on the short comings detected, has taken a back seat in the scheme of things. This is partly due to the hurried manner in which the schemes are executed. Political executives want quick results, as their term of office is too short. This has resulted in an administrative system, which is in a perpetual hurry. Emphasis is on speed, rather than quality. This frequently results in cutting corners. The proverbial man in a hurry has no time to look back. This is by and large the position of the administrative system. Moreover, with the tenure of the administrative officers being shorter than their political masters (on an average about less than an year), it is hardly possible to have any effective control on a sprawling field level organisation. Uncertainty of tenure acts as a damper on the exercise of adequate supervisory control. This has also eroded the effectiveness of higher administrative officers. The situation has made the subordinate field staff enormously powerful, at the same time vulnerable to abuse of power. The practice of line system in administration has virtually disappeared and each is left to his own device. The concept of collective responsibility has almost disappeared.

The cutting-edge staff, who are in fact the public face of the government, are left to their own device. They are required to take the decisions on the spot and have to work under considerable pressure. Most of the decisions are time bound and have to be taken quickly. This gives considerable scope for mistakes, as well as corruption. Moreover a person, who is aggrieved by a particular decision, even if rightly taken, sometimes nurses a grievance. The opportunity for appeal, being limited or time consuming, the decision becomes a *fait accompli* for most of the people. Fortunately for the administration, majority of the people do not go in for further litigation. As we well know, majority of Indians are law abiding and peaceful. But in all societies there are people, who think they are more equal than the others and demand priority treatment. In fact, these people work as a pressure group on field level functionaries. It may be said that these groups work as unofficial vigilante agencies on the officials and act as checks on arbitrary actions on their part. While this may be true to certain extent, in actual practice, these groups become unofficial and extra legal power centres. The officials want to be on the right side of such people and acquiesce to their demands and thus emboldened, neglect the common people, who are not in a position to raise their voices. This creates an imbalance in government services, where the rich and powerful are able to corner major portion of government services.

There has been a trend in recent times, where citizens have been organizing themselves to protect their rights. In 2008, there were widespread ration riots in West Bengal, leading to violent protests against the irregularities in the public distribution system. This has been mostly against the system, where the party apparatchiks in collusion with the government machinery were controlling the system. It is necessary that a better system is in place to protect the common man's interest. It is unfortunate that a system of patronage remains in the government delivery system. It is common experience that one can get his work done better and more expeditiously, if he has the right credentials or the right references. A system of VIPs (very important persons) which has developed over the years, clamouring for immediate attention impinges on the system. Once some citizens want to be more equal than the others and want to jump the queue, the problem starts.

A democratic administrative system must not be burdened with VIP syndrome, if it is to treat all citizens as equals. Unfortunately a feudal mindset, burdened with a colonial legacy, has resulted in a system of VIPs of different strata. Unless one is in one of these hallowed circles, it will be very difficult to get ones work done. It is necessary that the culture of VIP in public administration is kept to the minimum. Public administration is one field where everybody has to be treated as equal and the system of treating some more equal than the others, because of their clout with powers that be, creates a semi-feudal atmosphere. In the private sector, the problem does not arise. In the market economy, everybody is automatically graded according to his purchasing power, i.e., money power. In public administration, this is not possible and will be treated as corruption. Obviously, those who want a preferential treatment, devise methods to get through. Unless, steps are taken to put down this practice of preferential treatment, public administration will further degenerate.

Chapter - VIII

New Work Culture

Gone are the days, when the higher officials used to function from the splendid isolation of their offices, churning out lengthy notes, either by hand or dictation. This used to be a lengthy process, as everybody had to apply his mind to the problem at hand and work out his views independently, without any directive from any higher functionary.

Nowadays, meetings are regarded as panacea of all problems and constitute an important element in the functioning of the bureaucracy, particularly of the upper echelon. The importance of a functionary depends on the number of meetings attended by him. One finds the top officials rushing from one meeting to another.

The key to the efficient and impartial functioning of the Secretariat system lay in the right of each functionary, whether clerical or official, to express his views independently. One could take justifiable pride in a note well written. This also constituted the element of responsibility in any government decision. The concerned functionaries' notings were on the file and each was responsible for his own views. This process had evolved over a period of time and constituted an important part of the government system. The process is well illustrated in the following delightful story.

'In 1896, I was Deputy Quartermaster-General at Simla; then, perhaps still, one of the hardest worked billets in Asia. After a long office day, I used to get back home to dinner pursued by a pile of files three to four feet high. The Quartermaster-General, my boss, was a clever, delightful work-glutton. So we sweated and ran together for a while a neck and neck race with our piles of files, but I was the younger and he was the first to be ordered off by the doctors to Europe. Then I at the age of forty-three, stepped into the shoes and became officiating Quartermaster-General in India. Unluckily, the Government at that moment was in a very stingy mood. They refused to provide pay to fill the post I was vacating and Sir George White, the Commander-in-Chief, asked me to duplicate myself and do the double work.

My heart sank, but there was nothing for it but to have a try. The day came; the Quartermaster-General went home and with him went the whole of his share of the work. As for my own share, the hard twelve hours' task melted by some magic into the Socialist's dream of a six hours' day. How was that? Because, when a question came up from one of the Departments I had formerly been forced to compose a long minute upon it, explaining the case, putting my own views, and endeavoring to persuade the Quartermaster-General to accept them. He was a highly conscientious man and if he differed from me he liked to put on record his reasons - several pages of reasons. Or, if he agreed with me, still he liked to agree in his own words and to "put them on record". Now, when I became Quartermaster-General and Deputy-Quartermaster General rolled into one I studied the case as formerly, but there my work ended: I had not to persuade my own subordinates: I had no superior except the Commander-in-Chief, who was delighted to be left alone: I just gave an order - quite a simple matter unless a man's afraid: "Yes," I said, or "No".[1]

Even at that time, there seems to be impatience, tinged with ridicule, for this process of decision making. It is easier to give an order in terms of 'yes' or 'no', than pass a reasoned order. Decisions in such case will be personality based and arbitrary. This becomes an individual based procedure of working and not a system based one. Such a procedure is possible in an authoritarian organisation, rather than a democratic one. But, the moral of the story is that few have patience with an elaborate decision making process. We have to decide, whether, we want a quick arbitrary method or a system, where the matters are professionally examined. In case, we choose the former, there will hardly be any need for a professional bureaucracy. It is hardly possible to have a 'yes' or 'no' system of decision making in a democratic set up. But, even in a democratic set up, it is quite possible to subvert the system, while maintaining a facade of procedural formality.

Secretariat procedure of work is basically an interactive system. In this process, clerical staff had an important role to play, in that they had to cite previous precedent in the matter, if any. For citing such precedent, a precedent register had to be maintained and one had to consult it, at least in important cases. This practice has long been outdated and precedent cases are unlikely to be easily available in departmental archives or Record Rooms. There are no law reporters, as in the case of judiciary to record the administrative decisions and without a system of verification of decisions taken earlier in similar cases, the personal element in decision making will be dominant. It will also give rise to arbitrariness in the system. Precedent cases used to constitute an important part in administrative decision making, as in judicial decisions.

The Government is expected to be a continuous system and not supposed to be affected by individual predilections, howsoever brilliant an individual may be.

Rule of law has to be paramount, whether in administration or judiciary, in a democratic system. Precedents play an important part in judicial decisions and case law constitutes an important part in the arguments of the bar, as well as the decision of the bench. This prevents arbitrariness and adhocism. It also ensures rationality and continuity in the judicial system of decision making. The integrity of the judicial system has been maintained largely due to the fact that judicial decisions are not taken in closed-door meetings, but in open courts, where the petitioner, respondent, along with their lawyers are present. In the name of quick disposal of cases, the time tested procedure has not been abandoned. This has stood the judicial system in good stead and through all the political and social turmoil, it has come through comparatively unscathed.

Nowadays, most of the important government decisions are taken through meetings. Earlier meetings used to be called only in cases of emergencies, but at present meetings is the order of the day. No official day is complete without its quota of meetings, when the higher officials are busy with their parleys. One will be a sorry bureaucrat indeed, if he does not have his quota of daily meetings. These have the advantage of dispelling the monotony of official routine, with tepid tea and biscuits thrown in as a bonus. Tea constitutes the basic official drink and is served in style in important meetings by liveried retainers. Till the sixties, meetings were much less common than they are these days. Meetings were an exception rather than the rule, which it is in the present dispensation of government administration. Meetings generally used to be called only in times of urgency, as these were supposed to disturb the normal functioning of the office, keeping the officer away from his desk for a long time.

In the mid-sixties, when I joined the Government of Orissa, conferences and meetings with central government officers were rare and far between. As there was a non-Congress government in the state (1967-72), whereas centre was under Congress rule, the Chief Ministers were very particular in maintaining the federal structure of governance. They resented any central interference and were careful in seeing that the higher officers are not guided by their counterparts in the Central Government, particularly since they belong to the same service. Probably the suspicion upper most in their minds was, if the higher officers at the Centre and state form an informal network, it will be possible for Central Government to have more and more say in the matters of state government. They were careful in not having any Trojan horse in their government.

The old school of politicians were conscious of the fact that informal networking of officials, cuts across the authority of the elected government, as many of the important decisions are taken because of mutual understanding between officials. Officers are expected to function as individual entities and give their views independently. Once they are influenced by each other, independence of individual officials will be lost. Everybody is expected to record his views, 'without fear or favour'. In fact, these four words are the key to the independence of the bureaucracy. Once these are compromised, group mind takes over. It is well-known that groups are less rational than the individuals, who constitute them. The crowd or herd mentality takes over, even in a group of highly intelligent people.

Collectors' conference used to be a big event in the state administration. All concerned with the event use to wear a busy look for days prior to the meeting and used to rush to their boss's room with lengthy notes on the agenda for discussion in the meeting. The Departmental Secretaries used to assume that their respective departmental work in the district constitutes the highest priority work for the Collector. If any particular Secretary felt that a Collector had not given due importance to his department's work, he used to feel aggrieved and sometimes give vent to his feelings, if he had sufficient support at the top. Such instances were not very common, but one or two such cases, did occur in almost all the conferences. If the Secretary or the department was important enough in the scheme of things of the Chief Minister, the Collector used to be transferred to a desk job. Rarely, things happened in the reverse direction. Sometimes, when a number of Collectors complained that they were not getting clearance for their projects from a particular department, the Secretary concerned had to face the music. However, except for minor hiccups, the meeting used to end in an atmosphere of bonhomie, with the Chief Minister throwing a grand dinner for all the participants.

No major decisions were generally taken in these meetings and it was more an interaction of Collectors with the ministers and officials at the government level. It is also a good public relations exercise with the mandatory press briefings. There is also an element of putting the Collectors on their toes, that the Big Brother is watching them. Later, however, the meetings became more and more serious, with a competition in authoritarianism. Earlier these meetings were basically attempts by political executives to reach out to the Collectors and politicians being more egalitarian than bureaucrats, the atmosphere was one of congeniality. Once the bureaucrats took control over the meetings, it became more and more an exercise in power play.

There used to be a standing joke that the minutes of discussion of the Collectors' conference used to be prepared before the meeting. This is because the minutes of discussion are hardly a reflection of the discussions in the meetings. Minutes constituted a list of platitudes and instructions to Collectors, which are general in nature and are well known and have been issued in successive Collectors' conferences. No Collector would dare to come up with the actual problems, for fear of being branded defeatist and ruffling too many feathers. Problems at the ground level are in fact far too many to be sorted out in a formal meeting of a day or two. This will require a major administrative exercise in problem solving, through group discussions, case studies with reference to actual problems and such other detailed methodologies, which will hardly be possible in view of the busy schedule of the government machinery.

Everyone wants that the business should be carried on, without raising too many problems. The smarter ones bring up certain matters, which are palatable to the authorities and which have been informally discussed. Collectors, who have been able to spend the money allotted to them quickly, are commended and those who have been lagging behind in this expenditure race are warned. Needless to say that this type of race for increased expenditure, is hardly conducive for financial discipline. Any suggestion regarding central assistance is generally welcome, as it gives the state government an opportunity to shift the responsibility to the Centre.

Frequent meetings ensure that the higher officials are in touch with each other and this leads to the formation of an informal club and consequently an important power network. As group dynamics plays an important part in the government system, this type of groups constitutes an important power lobby. There is perhaps no organization anywhere which can said to be completely free from a system of informal associations amongst the members based on various factors like personal likings, social relations etc. Once, however, an informal network of authority develops, the formal network of authority may not function properly, creating a serious bias in the administrative system. In the UK such groups, based on old boys' network, had led to a severally restricted bureaucracy. In India with various social groups, based on caste, language-groups, etc, weightage of such a system of informal groups, will prove to be inimical to an efficient and impartial administration. In fact, the functioning of group within groups is a major danger to the efficient working of an impartial administrative system.

Panacea of Meetings

The Government work through meetings and committees apparently look to be more democratic and interactive method of decision making than decision taken through lengthy notings in files, for which few have patience these days. Although meetings are not an altogether new innovation in administration and have been there since the beginning, it has lately assumed greater importance and has worked as a panacea to cut through the proverbial red tape. In the process administration has become more subjective. It is hardly possible to take any objective decision amongst a room full of people. Decision in a group will be affected by group psychology, rather than individual rationality. It is common knowledge that individuals on their own can be expected to be basically rational, but when they are in a group, herd mentality takes over. Individuals, when in a group, basically submerge their rationality to be one with the group, which hardly tolerates any individual view, which is in variance with the group.

In today's administration, there is hardly any scope for any individualism or individual brilliance. A good bureaucrat should surrender his individual ego to the group and learn to think more like the group. Group ego replaces individual ego. One must think and act his part in a group, rather than as an individual. In this lies the art of bureaucratic salvation. As officialdom does not encourage any individualism, more and more officials are taking recourse to poetry and such other extra-curricular activities.

Meetings are also an important instrument for exercise of authority. The agenda of the meeting is drawn up by the top man and it is he who guides the meeting, either himself or through one or two of his trusted aides. Views on the subjects have mostly been preconceived earlier by the power hierarchy. This method cuts across the red tape and the official paraphernalia nicely and the political masters can be kept happy. Lengthy departmental consultations can be avoided in this way. This also makes most of the huge government machinery redundant. The Committee of Secretaries is all powerful and has effectively done away with the system of departmental consultations, which is the basis of the Secretariat pattern of administration. This has also introduced the element of authoritarianism in the system. One has to follow the boss, who knows the best. One has to learn to think like the boss, if one has to be successful in the rat race of bureaucracy.

Generally the meetings are to be held with sufficient notice and an agenda, but meetings are often held at short notices with an impromptu agenda. This is in fact a short cut to lengthy and inconvenient notings in the file. Once the problem is placed in the meeting, the views of the authority (minister or top bureaucrat) is made clear and it will be a foolhardy official indeed, who will write anything in the file against the subtle but firm directions of powers that be. In this way very little can be known from the files about the way a particular decision has been taken. This is a comparatively new trend in public administration, where it has become necessary to know the mind of the boss.

Earlier officials took justifiable pride in giving their independent views in the file. Well reasoned notes along with precedent cases quoted were the order of the day. Nowadays everybody is in a hurry and laboriously written notes have become outdated. In the electronic age, efficiency depends on decisions taken in a hurry and not after a detailed discussion in a file, where the contribution of each individual is recorded and one cannot back away from it. There can be no gainsaying the fact that decisions of public importance should be taken after due consideration. A wrong decision will cost the public exchequer heavily both in time and money, besides not serving the purpose for which it was intended.

In a meeting, the discussion is controlled by the boss and it is only his favourites or those with sufficient clout with higher authority, who get a chance to air their views. Others are reduced to the category of listeners to make up the numbers. For important meetings, there is generally a prior informal discussion, when the agenda items are formulated and the line of action in the proposed meeting is chalked out. Only after a blue-print for the meeting has been prepared that a formal meeting is called. Nobody is expected to speak out of turn in a meeting and woebegone the official, who indulges in such reckless adventurism. In case, one comes out with a view, which is in variance, one will be promptly cold shouldered with icy looks or ridicule. The Government meetings are not between equals, but between individuals at different levels of hierarchy. In such a situation free and fair discussion is hardly possible. Argumentative Indian does not exist in the bureaucracy.

Like the agenda, the proceedings of the meeting are also drawn up in the office of the chairman of the meeting. Recorded official proceedings do not reflect the detailed discussions and leave any inconvenient points, which might have been raised in the course of discussion. It can hardly be said to be a faithful reflection of the deliberations, which had taken place. Recorded official version of the meeting merely consists of the summary of the decisions on the issues which were required to be vetted in the meeting. In this situation, the official, who works as the secretary of the meeting and drafts the proceedings, becomes the most important person in the scheme of things, next to the chairman. Generally this job is entrusted to a comparatively junior officer, who enjoys the confidence of the chairman. The officer, who presides over the meeting, has little time for such routine work as drafting the minutes and is happy to leave it to his trusted subordinate, who relieves him of this tedium. Operative parts of any meeting are the recorded minutes of discussion and since this is the prerogative of the chairman and secretary of the meeting, most of the others merely lend their names to the attendance list.

Discussion in a meeting cannot be a substitute for detailed discussion in the file. These are little better than class room exercises. The presiding officer is the dominant presence and he sets the tone of the meeting. In most cases, he has already made up his mind and has called others about the urgency of implementing the decision and chalk out the line of action accordingly. In such cases these exercises are mere formalities and are called merely to rubber stamp the decisions already taken. In most cases decision in important matters, has already been taken informally in a small group and the meetings are called to implement the decisions of the authority.

Over the years, the government administration has become more and more authoritarian and less tolerant of individual views. Indian guru system is quite evident in the administration. If there is no guru, one has to be found. The boss or the top man generally takes the part of the guru. The Guru must have his disciples and so forms the different cordons of disciples round him. The Guru system does not tolerate any opposite view and complete surrender to the authority is called for. Decision in this system is not taken through free and frank discussions, but through dictats of the Guru. Now, from where he gets his thinking inputs to come to his decision, is another matter, but it is certainly not through open discussions. It is extremely dangerous, if such a trend takes place in public administration.

Subordination of the administrative system to an imaginary superior order, in the form of following the boss blindly will only encourage authoritarianism and is ill-suited for a democratic, responsible administration. The concept of questioning a government order within the system, even if one thinks that it is blatantly wrong, is akin to blasphemy in religion. Quite forgetting that it has emanated from a particular individual or group of individuals and a second look will not be to the detriment of the prestige or position of any individual or organization. In fact, when a decision is attributed to a group, it is very difficult to fix individual responsibility or liability of any particular individual. Decisions through meetings provide a convenient means of avoiding individual liability. It will be hardly possible to take action against an entire group. Role of the individual becomes amorphous in a group. Individual reasoning gets submerged in group thinking. But a group has hardly a mind of its own and it is the thinking of the dominant individual or coterie which counts. This method of operation opens the way to rule by coterie, which is one of the worst things that can happen in public administration.

The Influence of Private Sector

Till the early eighties, seniority used to be the single most important criterion in promotion of officials. The criteria for promotion were seniority cum merit, with seniority being the preponderant factor. Earlier there were some unwritten rules and ethos in civil service and respect for seniority was one of them. It was considered to be an upstar to try to supersede a person, who is senior in age and rank. One of the virtues of civil service was patience. One has to wait for one's turn. It was not the done thing to jump the queue. Promotions were also few and far between and it was not considered proper to deprive a senior person of his dues for which he has been waiting for years. It was realised over the years that supersession of officials on flimsy grounds, causes needless heart burning and demoralisation. In fact it causes more harm than good. The concept of merit is subjective, whereas seniority is a matter of fact. Seniority cannot be easily changed and is justifiable. Greater weightage of merit over seniority, shows greater importance of subjectivity over objectivity.

This ethos of civil service proved to be a hindrance for ambitious individuals, who were not willing to wait for their turn and were eager to jump the queue to prove their worth. By the eighties, public administration had come increasingly under the influence of the private sector work culture. It was thought that private sector work culture was much superior to work culture in the sphere of public administration and merit alone should be the criterion of promotion. There was also some loud thinking for introducing the concept of hire and fire. It was thought that introducing the private sector culture would make the bureaucracy much more accountable and efficient. Every organisation develops a culture of its own over the years. Organisational culture is more a matter of evolution than imposition. Public administration does not market services in the way private sector does. The basic difference between both these organisations needs to be realised, before the culture of one can be imposed on the other.

Private sector work ethos is person centric, where the power is concentrated in a single individual at the top of the ladder. The secret of success in such an organisation lies in catching the eye of the boss. This gives enormous power to a single individual. With public administration under attack for non-performance, it was thought that adopting the culture of the private sector, where one always looks upwards for direction, was the best way of bringing a radical change in the work culture. In the process, it was conveniently forgotten that the ambit of public administration has expanded enormously over the span of a few decades, without putting a formal system in place to tackle such enormous workload. A system, which was originally designed to handle land revenue administration, was suddenly saddled with the task of implementing the enormous political agenda of the party in government. With everybody in a hurry, there was little time for any systemic support for such increased workload and adhocism was resorted to. Needless to say that problems started from day one.

When desired results were not forthcoming and the higher officials were under attack from their political masters, they demanded greater powers over their subordinates. Now, in public administration, everybody is bound by rules and the concept of master and servant was not there, as the power of hire and fire was not their's, due to constitutional safeguards. In a rule bound system, interpretation of the rules is the prerogative of the individual concerned and his official superior has legally no say in the matter. This was in fact the greatest strength of the bureaucracy, which gave it independence, not only from external pressure, but also from itself, where a superior official could not pressurise a subordinate staff to put up a note to his liking. If he wanted to have his way, he had to overrule the latter in file.

I recollect, when I was Deputy Secretary in the state government, there was a proposal from a senior head of department for purchase of costly equipments and machinery, involving sizeable finance. For such expenditure, there was also no budget provision, which means there was no legislative sanction for such huge expenditure. Legislative sanction is mandatory for this. I pointed this lacuna in the file. There were also other procedural loopholes in the matter. Since the proposal did not satisfy the rules, this was rejected. The concerned

Head of Department, who was a senior officer, did not take kindly to this and wrote a strong letter to the Secretary, who was junior to him, that he had no control over his officials, who rejected his proposal. When the Secretary discussed the matter with me, I pointed out the position. He was however, not satisfied and did not want to displease the official, who had lot of clout. He asked me that the proposal should be passed the same day. I put up a note pointing the various legal difficulties in approving the proposal.

The Secretary was not too happy and asked the internal Financial Adviser to give a favourable note, which he obliged. After this, the Secretary had no difficulty in approving the proposal. I had however, the satisfaction of recording my views in the file. Incidentally, it may be said that the Financial Adviser was due for a promotion. About seven years later, when I became Head of Department in the same office, I found that the machinery purchased was defective and the establishment had no use for the same. Everybody had forgotten about the matter and it was a huge wastage of public funds. It was however, peanuts compared to the huge expenditure made in such wasteful purchases, which has become the rule rather than the exception. It was basically a clash of egos, where the senior officer could not condescend to have his proposal fairly examined. The system of check and balances was gradually *bid adieu*. I must say that such intolerance is more common among officials than politicians.

Pliable Bureaucracy

In the quest for a pliable bureaucracy, the Annual Charter Role (ACR) was found to be a most convenient tool. Article 311 of the Constitution of India prevents any arbitrary action against any civil servant of the Union or State, without due process of law. This article was not enacted by the constitution makers on merely humanitarian grounds, but to ensure the independence and morale of the civil service. They realised that a pliant and demoralised civil service was not desirable and will not be able to serve the nation properly. It was not so much the political establishment, but the bureaucracy itself, which took to the concept of committed bureaucracy with a great deal of zeal. There has been constant clamour in the bureaucracy for more and more power for control. Since any punitive action has to be according to due process of law and cannot be imposed arbitrarily, besides being appealable, the innocuous ACR, without any such provisions, has provided a powerful tool for bureaucratic control.

The higher civil services are pyramidal in their organisational structure and are promotion oriented. In such a situation ACR plays a crucial role. Absolute control over this hierarchical structure can be maintained through this single secret document. This single document has eroded the independence of bureaucracy, where everybody has to look upwards to the boss. It has also been costly in terms of organisational efficiency, as the strength of any organisation depends on the collective wisdom and efficiency of all the members and not a single member and his chosen followers. Public administration cannot afford to be person oriented. It has to uphold the rule of law and not rule of persons. Unless this is done, it will gradually turn into an oligarchic organisation.

Power Brokers

Decision making is an important part of the job of the higher civil service. It is necessary that decisions are fair and do not involve undue wastage of public funds. In view of this, it is necessary that there is a well-laid down procedure and those decisions are not ad hoc in nature. Time honoured procedure in government has been discussion in file through notings. The concerned officials are to give their independent views in writing, after examining pros and cons of the matter. This exercise helped in formulating a proper decision. This also ensured accountability in decision making. It made the decisions system oriented, rather than person oriented. This was however, not to the liking of many, who attributed it to red tapism. The system ensured a rule oriented bureaucracy, rather than a dictate oriented bureaucracy. It was also not suitable for favouring undue requests. This was also not to the liking of many, who were unwilling to have their cases properly examined. In fact, it was a serious hindrance for all sorts of patronage. It also helped in checking any undue pressure on the administrative machinery. It is an effective check on the common practice of using pressure tactics like 'I know your boss; I am related to such and such person'. Whereas, this is an easy and convenient method of getting ones job done, if one has friends or relations in high places in the government hierarchy, vast majority of persons, who have no such advantages, are left high and dry. This practice degenerates the system into patronage administration, rather than public administration. Cultivating contacts in the corridors of power, has gradually become an important methodology in dealing with the government machinery. It has also created a system of power brokers. In fact, patronage administration is a form of corruption, where the vast majority, who has no contacts, is treated as second class citizens. However, this is a form of corruption, which has attracted little or no attention from the society.

The system of independent notings in files, has not been bidden adieu completely but has been very much diluted by various methods. In all important matters, meetings are invariably called and the line of action required by the top authorities is made clear either explicitly or implicitly. After this, there is no question of any independent examination of the matter. One, who has not taken the hint, will be in for serious trouble. But there will be hardly anybody willing to be a martyr at the altar of officialdom. There is another way, in which official compliance is ensured. Departmental Secretaries in the Central Government are given the option to choose the senior officials, working under them. This gives a scope for patronage, for unless one is known to that particular official or has powerful connections, it will be difficult to get a berth in his department. Similar is the position with powerful secretaries in the state government. Once the secretary or the higher official gets officials of his choice, who are beholden to him, they will be hardly in a position to give any independent advice, which is not to the liking of authorities. All these are creating an oligarchic tendency in our civil services, in which personal loyalty counts more than organisational loyalty. This is destroying the very ethos of civil service.

Endnote

1. Herbert A Simon, A*dministrative Behavior. A study of Decision-making Process in Administrative Organization,* Macmillan Company, quoted from Sir Ian Hamilton, *The Soul and Body of an Army.*

Chapter - IX

Bogey of Corruption

Cornwallis, who had lost the American Empire of the British, sincerely believed that all Indians are corrupt and cannot be trusted with public service, when he became the Governor General of India. After having failed in America, he did not want to commit a mistake for the second time and wanted to keep India as a perpetual colony of Britain and this provided a convenient alibi. In fact Cornwallis's belief became the corner stone of British administration in India. Shortly after, we were able to shake off the British rule and started administering ourselves; we started suffering from the Cornwallis syndrome. No book on public administration in India can be taken seriously, unless corruption is discussed in some detail.

The view persists that Indian politicians are the most corrupt element in the society, followed by the bureaucracy. This provides the grist for gossip mills, from luxury hotels to the meanest tea houses. This is a national pastime, even better than cricket. The mention of the word corruption brings out the primeval instinct in the average Indian and rationality takes a backseat. It seems to be an all pervading phenomenon and the more we talk of it, the more we have of it. After the decline of socialism, it is not fashionable to begrudge the rich and their lifestyle, as the economists tell us that they contribute significantly to the growth of our GDP (Gross Domestic Product) and are playing a major role in making India an economic superpower. It is only political and administrative corruption, which is preventing us from achieving our true potential.

Within a period of few decades, many of our societal perceptions have undergone major changes, which have not happened in centuries. Less than a generation back, it was considered indecent by the majority of people to flaunt one's wealth. Even the rich were coy about displaying their wealth. But today things have changed and rampant consumerism has seized all of us, where flaunting one's wealth is the in thing. This, together with the mania of making a quick buck, has completely overhauled our morals in our quest to get rich quickly. This has affected all sections of the people. The problem of corruption is basically a societal one and should be analysed in a broader perspective, instead of simply treating it as a bureaucratic malaise. We cannot expect a corruption-free society, just as we cannot expect a crime-free one. Even in the most prosperous and developed countries, there will be people, who are keen to get an undue benefit and if the same is not a marketable commodity or service, will try to obtain the same through illegal means and thus set the ball of corruption rolling. No country is free from this problem.

Poorer countries will have more of this problem, as goods and services are limited and cannot be entirely left to the market forces, since it will deprive the people in lower economic segments from gaining access to the same. Full play of market forces will play havoc in a society with great inequality of income and where a large majority of people live below the poverty line. It is widely believed that earlier higher levels of bureaucracy were comparatively free from corruption and the malaise was limited to the lower levels, particularly the field functionaries in police and revenue. Today this seems to have pervaded all levels and no section of the society can be said to be free from it. Problems of administration are zeroed in on this phenomenon more than anything else. This widespread phenomenon is fast eroding the confidence of the people in a fair and impartial administration.

Most of the people are sensible enough not to subscribe to such extreme views and have no difficulty in transacting their day to day business vis-à-vis the administrative machinery. It is only the extremes which attract the popular attention and provide juicy material for marketable stories. It will be quite unfair to tar the honest hardworking public servant, which most of them are, due to the misdeeds of a few.

Corruption in its present form has its genesis in government contracts and food rationing, brought about by the Second World War from 1939. India was the staging ground for troop and armament movement to South East Asia, in the war with Japan. Large-scale construction work was necessary for building up military facilities like aerodromes, roads for movement of troops and equipments, barracks for housing of troops and storage depots. All these works had to be done in a hurry and quality was compromised. In the beginning of the War, the military assessment was that India may become a major theatre of battle, as Japanese troops were fast approaching India and had already captured Burma and Singapore. The turn of events changed, once the USA was drawn into the war. The Japanese arms and personnel got engaged with the Americans in Philippines, China, Korea and various islands near Japan.

Threat to India from Japanese war efforts ceased, within a short span of a few months. But the war effort in the form of construction work continued, as it was being financed by the Indian public. The building of major war facilities were being financed by the Indian Government through deficit budget, which necessitated large-scale increase in currency. This created a major inflationary situation and shortages of essential commodities, as hoarding of these commodities was resorted to. The result was the Bengal famine of 1942-43. However, these facilities, which were mostly not required or were under utilized, proved to be a great source of profit for war time contractors and their government beneficiaries. Since, these were temporary works, meant for a possible war, which never materialised, nobody was interested in the quality of job done. Consequently, the contractors raked in huge profits.

The Government contracts became an important source of business activity from 1940 onwards. Huge projects taken up at public cost with execution being entrusted to private enterprise opened the flood gates of corruption. The ethos of private sector and government are different. Whereas, the former is there basically for profit and not for social service, government's professed motive is service. This has produced a situation of worst of both the worlds, where both parties try to enrich themselves. It is, however, an established fact that projects cannot be executed by government agencies, which are rule bound. Rules act as an impediment to execution of project, where decisions have to be taken on the spot. Rules are based on preconceived ideas and experience and provide little scope for discretion. As government records are open to inspections and audit, these have to be kept within rules and no sensible officer would like to be caught on the wrong foot. The contractors being nongovernment agencies have more flexibility in these matters. It is this flexibility, which is essential for execution of projects. However, once any liberty with rules and regulations are taken, one is treading on dangerous grounds and the doors of corruption are being gradually opened.

It is not often realized that corruption is a two-way phenomenon and there are two parties to any transaction. Unless somebody is willing to pay for some undue favour, there will be no corruption and it will die a natural death. In view of this, it should be treated more as a societal problem than a purely administrative one. When the social norms decline, bureaucracy, being a part of the society is bound to be affected by this malaise. For every corrupt bureaucrat, there has to be a similar number of people, who stand to gain by breaking the rules. The nexus between the corrupt elements within the bureaucracy and outside is posing a serious problem. Bureaucratic corruption is only the tip of the iceberg of a huge parallel economy, which has emerged over the years. This parallel economy has grown on government funds gone astray and now poses a major challenge. Steps to control this sector have not yielded any appreciable results.

Money has no colour and can hardly be distinguished as black or white, once it is circulating in the economy. Laws of economics are the same for the parallel economy, as also the regular economy. Moreover, the distinction between the two is not clear and they merge in many points. This makes the two indistinguishable. In such a situation, it is difficult for the government to start a witch hunt in the matter, without hurting the economy of the country. Morality and economics do not always go hand in hand.

Practice better than Sermons

There is the well known story of a proverbially honest politician, who was in some financial problem, being offered a substantial sum of money for a small favour by an established businessman. As usual he refused and ticked off the bribe giver. The person concerned, who was known to the politician, tried to convince him by telling, 'Sir, please accept the amount as a gift. Nobody else will know. I don't want any favour.' The reply was, 'My friend, I will at least know and I will have to live with myself, so please don't embarrass me'. The story is generally attributed to Lal Bahadur Shastri. It is typical of Shastri, in that he did not take any high moral grounds and did not humiliate the person concerned, but simply reminded him that what he was doing was wrong. I, for one, will attribute the statement, as being typical of Sri Shastri, having had the opportunity to meet him for a short time, during our visit to the Prime Minister, as IAS trainees in December 1965, a week before he went to Tashkent to meet a tragic end. He made it a point to interact with all the trainees and did not offer any sermons. I still remember that the Prime Minister made it a point to sit in the same type of chair as the trainees. He did not think it necessary to sit in a throne like seat to increase his prestige or create a sense of majesty.

This was in sharp contrast to our meeting with the Home Minister, Gulzarilal Nanda, the previous day at Hyderabad House, New Delhi. At that time, Home Ministry was also dealing with the Personnel Department and the All India Services were also within its portfolio. The training institute, National Academy of Administration, was under the administrative jurisdiction of this Ministry. In view of this, the meeting with the Home Minister was an important official one and not merely courtesy call. When we went to the venue at the scheduled time, to our surprise, there was nobody to receive us. Obviously, the meeting was a low priority one for the Home Ministry. After some time, somebody came and told us that the Minister was busy with some important affairs of the state and we will have to wait. After waiting for some time, we were taken to a huge hall bereft of any furniture, save a throne like chair and asked to wait for the Minister. Ultimately Sri Nanda arrived. It was an embarrassing occasion, as Sri Nanda was courteous enough not to immediately occupy the seat, with all of us, including the Director and staff members kept standing. He exchanged a few words with us to the effect that he was extremely busy and had to come from an important meeting. Somebody from the Directorial staff volunteered and the chorus was taken up by others that we will be happy to sit on the floor and the Minister may kindly occupy the chair. He was happy at this sign of humility on our part and that we are learning to be good bureaucrats. He was gracious enough to say that a few more chairs could have been arranged, but since this has not been done, we will have to make the best of the situation. Sri Nanda was well-known for his honesty and he offered us a few platitudes on honesty and probity in public life, but no tea. It seems unlikely that hundred odd chairs and tea could not be arranged for the Home Minister's meeting, scheduled well in advance. Sri Nanda was probably teaching us the first lesson to be a good bureaucrat.

Sri Shastri did not think it necessary to teach us anything and treated us as human beings, not subordinates. I think, we learnt more from this brief interaction than anything in our long and ad hoc training programmes. One cannot achieve importance by humiliating others and respect breeds respect. In this respect Sri Shastri was certainly a unique personality and his untimely demise was a serious loss to India. He had the vision to realize that these young men and women will be in position of authority for next three decades or more and if they are treated well by the highest functionary in the country they will do the same to others in their turn. This is an intrinsic quality of leadership and cannot be learnt from business school. Sri Shastri had neither been to Harvard Business School nor to Oxford or Cambridge, those citadels of knowledge, but I am sure he could have occupied the post of Dean in Man Management in any of these institutions.

It is a well known human psychology that generally persons who have been well treated when at the receiving end of the authority, tend to reciprocate the same. In the bureaucratic system, everybody is either a superior or a subordinate at the same time. The lower officials, particularly those at the executing end have tremendous power over the people and if they are bullied by their official superiors, they are likely to do the same to the citizenry. The fear of punishment on complaint is not deterrent enough for such behaviours. Even the clerical staff, whose contact with the people is limited to files, is likely to get a vicarious pleasure by their tyranny over files. The government machinery has to be more democratic and less authoritarian, if it has to serve the common man.

I am not sure, however, whether the Shastri School provides a better recipe to be a successful bureaucrat or the Nanda School. In the complex individual psyche, largely created by society, power and authority play a big part. These are the primeval instincts, which have been nurtured by society since ages. According to some, for the authority to be effective, its manifestations must be visible. Authority must have grandeur to create a sense of awe for those on the other side. This view has become more and more prevalent today, than at any time earlier. Today the concept of status is being guarded by a posse of armed policemen, in the name of security, as if the common man does not require any security at all. A new class of VIPs has emerged, which is certainly an anathema in a democratic society. Obviously, some are considered more equal than the others. The concept of equality of men is certainly outdated in today's democracy.

It is one of the drawbacks of modern life that we go more by form than substance. We have preconceived notions about most of the things and judge others by the same. The modern society is an opinionated one and we too often make judgments about individuals and situations on ad hoc basis, which we regret sometime later. Human relation is more and more becoming a casualty in today's market driven society. Our interaction is more as a buyer and seller of goods and services and not as an individual. Individual identity is submerged under the guise of a commercial person.

As in the story/incident, individual's conscience is the best guide, whether a particular act is right or wrong. It is not the fear of punishment which prevents a person from doing something wrong. It will not be possible for the state to provide so many laws and a supporting number of law enforcement agencies to guard all delinquencies. Moreover, the law enforcers are from the same social milieu, there is no guarantee that they will not fall a victim to the very same temptations. We will then have a system of 'to set a thief to catch a thief'. However, every individual has a conscience to guard himself, against any wrong doing on his part. In a fast moving globalized consumer society, where a person is treated more as a commodity than an individual, such a concept is becoming more and more obsolete. In today's market driven society, individual conscience does not count for much and one who can bend the rules favourably according to circumstances, without breaking them, proves successful and can climb the economic and social ladder. Great social and economic disparities cannot be explained by anything else. It is unlikely that more than ninety-five percent of the population is so qualitatively inferior from the top five per cent.

Who is to Blame – Individual or System?

It is also necessary to analyze whether the problem is a systemic one or due to individual truancy. Good administrative machinery should not leave too many loopholes in the system, which can be exploited. The plethora of laws and rules create a complicated situation for the average citizen. We think that all the ills of the society can be solved by simply laying down rules. Many times the laws are drafted in a hurry and the legislatures are not given sufficient time also to study the same. Most of these rules require frequent amendments, making it even more difficult for execution. Minutes of discussion of the Parliament or any State legislature would show that very little time is spent on detailed discussion of the bills and only few are referred to select committees. Most of the acts involve technical matters and proper justice to them, can be done in select committees only. Hurrying through legislation on the ground of administrative expediency denies the legislature adequate opportunity to examine the same and the exercise becomes more an executive one.

Laws are executed by the bureaucracy and more the number of laws, more powerful the bureaucracy. Today's society requires more and more laws to control itself, as the social norms are fast breaking down under the impact of consumerism among other forces. Society requires more and more laws to protect itself from the conflicting interests of its members. When interests of individuals conflict, laws are required to prevent chaos. The need of enactment of more and more laws is a clear indication that social conflicts and tensions are on the rise. This has created an over-dependence on the bureaucratic system. More laws mean a more regulated society. Over dependence on bureaucracy has the effect of drying up social initiative and responsibility, which are the hallmark of a free society. A society has to be self-governing to a greater extent and not be hamstrung by an omnipresent bureaucracy. Need for bureaucracy and bureaucratic intervention has to be exception, rather than the rule. A society must develop trust amongst its constituent units to be a homogenous entity and not be 'an unorganized aggregate of disunited peoples'! (The portion within quote is Mirabeau's description of pre-revolutionary France of 1789.) (Jacques Gernet, *A History of Chinese Civilization* p.28)

An acquisitive society is the breeding ground for corruption. Over the years, society has become more and more consumer oriented and keeping up with the Joneses has become the in thing. Consumerism has spread to all sections of the population and bureaucracy has been no exception. Earlier, the basic ethos of bureaucracy was middle class value system, which frowned on ostentation. If anybody indulged in a life style beyond his means, it attracted immediate criticism and disapprobation from his colleagues and such a person was treated as a black sheep. Social sanction amongst the peers, against anybody indulging in corruption, was the greatest insurance for prevention of corruption. The morality factor is also missing with 'making a quick buck' being the guiding factor in today's society. In modern day society, religious factor of 'fear of God' is hardly a deterrent against corruption. The system of secret donations to religious institutions is also designed to assuage the individual conscience and to buy divine forgiveness, whether real or imaginary. Religious institutions also encourage such donations. They are obviously, very much part of the market system and do not want to miss out on the economic largesse. Earlier, all these factors were in place and 'fear of God', as well as fear of societal condemnation, acted as checks on wrong doing and corrupt practices.

With huge amount of public funds being channelised through the government machinery for various development and poverty alleviation programmes, the problem of misuse and diversion of government funds, have become a major problem today, threatening the very democratic structure of the society. The problem of corruption surfaced in a big way in the public delivery system with the foodgrains rationing system, introduced for the first time during the shortage situation created by the Second World War and continued after independence. There was no going back on the system, as the government could not afford another Bengal Famine. The shortage situation continued during the initial years of independence, leading to black marketing and hoarding. This caused large scale public outcry, forcing Prime Minister Jawaharlal Nehru to make the statement that 'black marketeers and hoarders should be hanged from the nearest lamp post'.

Nowadays, of course, hoarding has become legal with large scale forward trading in commodities. Trading in future derivatives is a product of market reforms, where prices can be controlled by the traders by skewing the market mechanism in their favour. The consumers are at the receiving end of this exercise of legal market manipulation, which is in fact hailed as a great business innovation. It is interesting to note how fast social morality changes. Price control is considered as an outdated relic of socialism and control raj. Any attempt by government to hold back prices is considered synonymous with England's King Canute's attempt to hold back the sea from advancing. Social perceptions in these matters have undergone a complete circle of change and speculation and forward trading and trading in future derivatives are major architectural pieces of the new economy ushered in by the reforms process.

It has been widely held that funds for rural development and poverty alleviation schemes are not benefiting the target group and there is large scale leakage of such funds. The Government machinery has been generally held responsible, since funds are channelised through it. But, now the fact remains that the executing bureaucracy does not work in isolation and has to work through available local entrepreneurs. Due to lack of proper entrepreneurship at the local level many of the schemes languish and are not completed within the stipulated period. This also leads to poor quality of execution. As most of these schemes are financed by the Central Government, there is considerable delay, before the funds reach the executing level. There are plethora of reasons for poor execution and consequent wastage and leakage of funds, which need be carefully and impartially examined.

It is now clear, that poverty cannot be eliminated by simply pouring in money in rural areas. Money has a tendency to gravitate to the rich and powerful, making them richer and more powerful. Economic logic favours them and not the poor. As a class of local entrepreneurs has to be developed for execution of the schemes, people, who are better organised and higher on the social ladder would be of great help. In fact, large scale pumping of money in rural areas has created serious economic imbalance. Rural poor has further been disempowered by large scale transfer of their assets, like land holdings to the richer elements, through legal or illegal means. Even traditional water rights have ceased through commercialisation of water bodies. Land Reforms (reform of land tenure system) have hardly made any impact, mostly due to adequate legal support. The general picture is one of economic disempowerment of the poorer sections of the society, for which they are hardly in a position to stand up for their rights and avail of the benefits being offered by the various government projects.

Executing agencies have been generally blamed for poor performance and for good intentions going haywires. This is not a correct perception of things. Lack of coordination between different levels of government is a major problem. While formulating the details of execution of a scheme, the cutting edge staff needs to be consulted and taken into confidence. All the schemes emanate from the national capital or the state capital and as such do not take into account the variations in local conditions. 'Planning from below', which was a major concept in the early stage of planning through involvement of panchayat bodies, is hardly taken seriously these days. Unless there is greater local involvement, schemes, however well drawn out are unlikely to be successful. There is also need for greater involvement of beneficiaries in the schemes through the abolition of the middleman system.

It is, however of utmost importance that these schemes are not scrapped on the ground of allegations of corruption, as is being urged by the market lobby. We have precedent of this from United Kingdom, when the poor laws were scrapped in the middle of the nineteenth century on the ground of corruption and mismanagement. Needless to say, this created further deprivation for the poor. The problem was alleviated by conquering colonies of emigration, like Australia. We have no such luxury and any discontinuance of poverty alleviation scheme will spell disaster.

Crying Wolf frequently will hurt the Poor

There are number of reports by different non-governmental bodies about corruption in various government programmes, particularly in the field of poverty alleviation schemes, conceived by the politicians. The so called facts brought out are mostly unsubstantiated and based on hearsay evidences. These reports are mostly meant for creating shock effects and give a wake-up call to the government. They also provide ammunition to the opposition to put the government on the dock. However, in the absence of specific information, no constructive debate in the matter takes place and the discussions are mostly confirmed to allegations and counter allegations.

Reports of these non-governmental agencies generally constitute a catalogue of misdeeds by government agencies. Most of these allegations are vague and do not help in fixing any responsibility on any body and constitute of only generalities. The point is, however, well taken that there is a big gap between expectations and performance. The corruption and leakage in public sector delivery system are used as weapons against the poverty alleviation schemes. Socialism has become a dirty word today and socialistic measures of government are held up for ridicule and a sign of inefficiency of the government machinery. *Wall Street Journal* (Asia Edition. Oct.18, 2007), came out with a news item 'How not to Help India's Rural Poor', castigating National Rural Employment Guarantee Act, 2006 which is to provide 100 days of work every year to every rural household. Two reports quoted in the news item are from Delhi based society for participatory Research in Asia and Centre of Environment and Food Security (CEFS).

It is of interest to note that number of expert bodies on government policy analysis and programme evaluation have come up to keep a close watch on government's activities. There has, however, no similar development to keep a watch on the activities of non-government sectors, although it is largely financed by public money. There has been little or no study on the activities in the stock market, although it deals with public money in the form of funds from public sector banks, where huge amount of government funds are parked. Stock market, which is one of the pillars of the private sector, remains a grey area for a large body of academics and an area of total darkness for the majority of the people. It is only a few operators associated with the stock market, who knows the nitty-gritty of the same. It is they who can put the entire financial system of the country at ransom, as was well illustrated with the various stock market scams, which followed the market liberalization and reforms process. There has been no indepth study of the working of stock markets. It is only when there is a major stock market crash, that there are some startling news item, after which the entire matter dies down. The modern private enterprise does not work with money of the poor, but with the money of the society, with loans from banks, which function with depositors and government money. There is also no detailed study by any private expert body of the working of government schemes regarding export subsidies. Most of the studies by private expert bodies relate to the government's policy alleviation schemes.

The report by CEFS (Centre for Environment and Food Security) is most striking and concludes that about 75% of funds in the scheme in Orissa has been siphoned and pocketed by the government officials. Quoting the CEFS report, the *Wall Street Journal* (Asia Edition, October, 18, 2007) goes onto say 'out of a total $187 millions in public monies spent in the State during the 2006-2007 fiscal year, around $127 million was effectively stolen'. The generalization is indeed striking, but hardly any details as to where the money has been channelised, is available. These types of reports generally generalise from particulars and tend to go to town without ascertaining all the facts. Reports drawn up on unverified facts and on hearsay evidence, placed before international readership, creates an impression that the entire bureaucracy specialized in corruption. If corruption on such a scale is possible in a single year, many of the bureaucrats would have figured in the Forbes' list of the billionaires. It is highly unlikely that such large scale corruption could have taken place with people's representative in place at different levels.

It is also strange that no sooner had the scheme been launched, than the crusade against corruption in implementing it had also been launched. Before the scheme could be properly grounded and all the modalities of its working been worked out, crusaders against corruption became active. The report was contested by the state government, but the organizations had already formed their views and did not enter into any dialogue with the Government, before making the report public to discredit the scheme. The intention of these organizations might have been good in that they genuinely wanted to help the people in getting their dues from the government. But the result has been the opposite.

The opponents of the poverty alleviation scheme have found in these reports, a convenient alibi for discrediting all such schemes, which have popular mandates, being passed by duly elected bodies. *Wall Street Journal,* which is the mouthpiece of market capitalism, immediately gave it wide publicity, without verifying all the facts. According to them any Government scheme which defies the so-called market logic by targeting the economically weaker sections should be immediately scrapped. In fact, this scheme has gone a long way in empowering the economically weaker sections in the rural areas. This is certainly not to the liking of the rural power elite. Unlike distributing doles and charities, these types of schemes are proactive and aimed at correcting social imbalance, particularly in rural areas and stop distress migration from rural areas. Social justice cannot be achieved without economic empowerment. In a sovereign democratic country, a citizen, whether rich or poor, cannot depend on charities - whether foreign or indigenous, religious or secular.

If the government is not able to muster through public recruitment policies, an army of officials, who are reasonably honest with their salary and perks, it is unlikely that any other agency can make a better job of it. Schemes are executed through panchayat bodies, which are elected by a due process and executed by people, who are recruited through open advertisement by a process of selection. They represent a large cross-section of people, who could not have entered into a conspiracy of corruption. These private investigation bodies could hardly have mustered any superior quality of persons to do concurrent physical audit of the job in such a short time. Most of these private investigating bodies have an agenda of their own. The 'holier than thou' approach is tendentious. Nobody can lay claim to absolute honesty and integrity in the present complex world. No society or organization can claim to represent the civil society, simply because of the fact that they operate outside the government system.

Wall Street Journal goes on to say 'The National Rural Employment Guarantee Act is symbolic of everything that's wrong with India's approach to economic reform. What's needed is not grand gestures and more handouts, but a comprehensive review of how to stimulate private investment and entrepreneurship. Mr. Gandhi (Rahul Gandhi) should understand that there is no better guarantee of employment than economic growth'. The regime of market friendliness initiated since 1991, has not been friendly to the poor in India. The various human development index figures compiled by the United Nations indicate an increase in poverty in absolute terms. The Prime Minister has gone on record as saying that the coming years are likely to witness a serious food shortage. Once this happens, the lowest income group will suffer the maximum. The food self-sufficiency which we had attained over years of post-independence planning has been frittered away in the course of a decade and a half. Market reforms carried out as per the directions of the trinity of economic wisdom, IMF, World Bank and WTO, have resulted in diversion of huge funds to non-productive sectors like speculation, entertainment and non-essential services. Deprived of funds, both public and private, agriculture sector has languished, after taking a backseat in the reforms process.

There is perhaps no greater proof of increasing poverty level than large-scale migration of rural poor to urban conglomerates. Large numbers of people in the rural areas have been marginalized, due to drying up of the flow of funds in agriculture and allied activities in the post-liberalization area. With the opening of the market economy, funds have found their way to non-productive activities like stock market speculation, service and entertainment activities. The economic reforms have catapulted India to the top of the billionaire list, with a growth figure of 8% and above, at the same time it has put India somewhere near the bottom in human development index. Scarcity of essential items, particularly foodgrains, have made a huge impact on the below poverty line population and hunger index has gone up steeply. When there is a competition between different economic activities non-essential items, which can muster greater profits than essentials like agriculture and allied activities with lower margin of profits, get priority. Indian Cricket Control Board is the richest in the world, while the Indian agriculture is languishing.

Economics is yet to find any answer to the problems of agriculture, because it is heavily loaded in favour of industry and ancillary activities. This is particularly so, as it is a product of British industrial revolution, which completely destroyed the traditional agricultural base in Great Britain. In spite of being a major colonial power, England was a country of rootless poor people as is clear from the writings of contemporary authorities, particularly Charles Dickens. Poor laws enacted to support the indigent population, were inadequate to support these people and were also being questioned as being badly administered and a waste of public money. The criticism of anti-poverty schemes echoes the opposition to anti-poverty laws.

With the economic and consequent social upheavals going on in India today, there is no going back for a popularly elected government on implementing employment generation and anti-poverty schemes on fudged economic logic. Further, so-called reforms in the form of commercialization of agriculture will spell disaster for the rural economy and will lead to further disempowerment of the poor. As scams and frauds in the stock exchanges and banks, cannot be grounds for doing away with these institutions, problems of corruption cannot be a ground for doing away with these vital schemes of social security. Solution to the problem of leakage of funds lies in plugging the various loopholes in the mechanism. Constant review of the working of the schemes and improvement of the delivery mechanism on the basis of experience gathered, are essential for better results. The problem is not simply a moral one, but an economic one. Poverty alleviation schemes basically represent a conflict situation between the social conscience of the government with the market forces. Since the market logic does not favour the economically marginalised section of the population, government has little choice in the matter and political will must prevail over economic logic. Of course, if the successful operation of these schemes can empower the people in a future date, market logic may change with better balance of economic forces.

There is need to take a holistic approach towards the problem of corruption, instead of a confrontational one. It is also thoroughly unfair to come to a conclusion and then publicise it that any agency or person is involved in any illegal act like siphoning away of public funds, without ascertaining all the facts. In many of the cases, it has been found that such reports are based on a wrong perception of government's accounting rules and procedures. Every organization has its own particular accounting procedure according to its requirements, which is difficult to be understood by the uninitiated. The accounting procedure in any large organization is bound to be complex and one must have a complete knowledge of the same, before taking up an audit of the same, whether officially or unofficially. There is a tendency to treat these things frivolously and with disdain.

The Government accounting procedures are supposed to be the epitome of red tapism to the uninitiated and are ridiculed, quite forgetting that these rules and procedures had evolved over a period of time to ensure that there is no leakage of public funds. Doing away with a large portion of checks and balances have made the system vulnerable, but even then unlike private organizations working with public funds, government organizations have to be much more transparent. Particularly due to the involvement of large number of stake holders and constantly working under public gaze. A demoralized bureaucracy will weaken the state machinery and consequently the polity. The state machinery can hardly function in an atmosphere of constant distrust. An atmosphere of trust and confidence needs to be created for effective functioning of a public administrative system. Good work done by the officials, particularly at the cutting edge level needs to be properly showcased and recognized. The efficiency of any organization depends on the performance of the persons, who directly operate the delivery system and interact with its clientele. For the government organization, this constitutes the society at large. Such a diverse clientele poses problems of its own and uniformity of satisfaction cannot be ensured. In such a situation, there are bound to be dissatisfied people, who demand from the system, more than their due. This, in fact, is the basic point of conflict.

A Case of over-zealousness gone awry

The role of the Collector assumes great significance during times of emergency, as he is supposed to function as the chief fire-fighter. As such occurrences are sudden and unexpected, it is hardly possible to have any standing ready made mechanism to deal with all kinds of emergencies, and lot of improvisation has to be made in such occasions. This calls for quick and on the spot decisions on matters, which are not always within the legal ambit of the Collector. He has to engage non-government agencies and private contractors to procure materials and distribute the same amongst the affected people. In most of these cases, rules cannot be strictly followed and ad hoc decisions have to be taken.

Woe betides the Collector, who fails to take prompt decisions in the matter and goes strictly by rules. He will be promptly disgraced and his official career will take a severe down turn. Adhocracy has to be the order of the day in tackling emergencies. In such a situation, the Collector has to take the bulk of the decisions, as being the man on the spot, for which he becomes vulnerable at a later stage. It is not possible to check the credential of all the contracting agencies and non-officials taking part in relief and rehabilitation work. In such a situation, where rules take a back seat, corruption cannot be ruled out. Moreover in works executed in a hurry, the quality naturally suffers, which sometimes becomes an open invitation to corruption.

A few years back a case was reported, in which a young Collector, a qualified medical practitioner, had done commendable work in providing relief to the affected people during a major flood in Bihar in 2004. His work was also internationally acclaimed and the *'Time'* magazine extolled him in a feature article as a model young executive in a state government. He was also winner of

Time Magazine's "Young Asian Achiever Award". For a junior officer from a backward state like Bihar to make it to an international prestigious American magazine for the right reason is little short of miracle. Generally the reportings are highly critical and praising a government official is the rarest of the rare occurrence. Such high profile projection is potentially dangerous for a government official, particularly if he does not have the right connections.

As things developed further, it became a sort of Pyrrhic victory. The officer got into trouble in less than an year, when there was a change of government in the state, with a vigilance probe into the utilisation of funds during the relief operations. It was found that some of the private agencies engaged by him in relief work had indulged in large-scale misappropriation and corruption. Among the 28 accused persons, there were two influential politicians, one being the brother of the Ex-Chief Minister. In relief operations during disasters, politicians cannot be ignored and will have a role to play as peoples' representative. Relief operation is not a simple administrative exercise, but has strong political overtones.

The kingpin of the operation was a small time businessman, with affiliation to an important political party. He operated through two fake firms and according to his own admission was the major beneficiary. Logistics of relief operations require instant and huge mobilisation of men and materials to provide immediate succour to the affected people. Any delay in providing relief will be seriously viewed by the government, the public and the press. Such huge quantities of materials and transport facilities are not immediately available and arrangements have to be made with distant and unknown sources. This provides an opportunity to fly by night operators, with connections in the right places, who are keen to cash in on the desperation of the administration. Now most of these persons had powerful backers and in most cases the officers are forced to accept such recommendations, as these come from political or administrative superiors.

The responsibility squarely rests with the officer and he becomes a scapegoat in this drama. In most of these cases, it takes years to file a charge sheet and even more time to get a conviction. In the meantime the life and the career of the official are ruined. There is no systemic support for such emergencies, where the administration of the entire country or even of the state can function as a single entity to provide relief to the affected area. These matters are treated, more as emotive issues, rather than administrative problems. The entire issue becomes a turf war between local administration, politicians and the press. In this particular case, the officer seemed to have controlled the turf war well and had come up as a hero. But obviously there were others, who had not taken too kindly to the episode and the victory was short lived with the change in official dispensation. Within a course of less than an year, from a hero, he became a villain. His fair weather friends deserted him and his official superiors, who should have pointed out the alleged irregularities and are equally guilty for lack of supervision and should have been fully accountable, escaped scot-free. They were not probably too unhappy that the official concerned has been taught a lesson for his upcoming and daring to corner all the credit.

The entire episode throws up a few uncomfortable questions. Administrative system functions on group responsibility and a system of checks and balances. These age old administrative practices have been *bid adieu* in the name of expediency. This is more of a systemic failure than anything else. The age old system of public finance is that no single official is kept in complete charge of state funds. According to Central Public Works Code, there is a separate line agency controlling the finances, with Chief Finance & Accounts Officer at the apex level, down to the Divisional Accountant at the Division level, the lowest independent executing agency. This is the basic norm for all executing agencies.

Entrusting a single officer with the responsibility of drawing and disbursing huge amount of public funds, without proper checks and balances, is against all canons of public administration. In the present case, the person concerned was purely unlucky, as there was change of government within a course of less than an year. It can safely be said that had there been no change of government, the relief operations conducted by the previous government, would not have been subject to vigilance probe and the officer would have gone on for higher things. The Collector is often used as a cat's paw in a bigger game.

The official concerned met a tragic end due to a disease contracted while being incarcerated as an under trial. The person all through claimed his innocence and nothing was proved against him in a court of law. But he seems to have been punished through extra judicial methods. His relations alleged that he contracted the disease due to the negligence of the jail authorities. This type of selected witch hunting has become a trend in administration, particularly when there is a change in government. Needless to say, that this is greatly eroding the morale of administration. Perhaps, the only sensible thing to do in such circumstances is not to play to the gallery too much and be a party to anybody's machinations. Trying to curry favour with the bosses should also be avoided. As in all human affairs, one's conscience and commonsense should be the only reliable guide in such matters.

The malaise of corruption in bureaucracy can be solved only by strengthening the system itself and not by fear of punishment or by any external agency. The fear factor has not acted as much of a deterrent, in spite of enactment of stringent anti-corruption laws. It is well known that even the best drafted law has loopholes, which can be taken advantage of by clever individuals, who want to bend the system for personal benefits. Moreover, fear is a negative emotion and is hardly conducive to efficiency.

Dismantling the earlier system of checks and balances with the ostensible purpose of cutting through the proverbial red tape has not served the administrative system well. While needless delay in urgent public matters cannot certainly be brooked, a reasonable amount of time is certainly required for proper formulation and analysis of any proposal, before it can take the shape of a government scheme and put into effect. It should not be a case of 'act in haste and repent later'. However, what is a reasonable amount of time should be specified and should not be left to individual whims and fancies. Most of the government decisions are quasi-judicial in nature and hence cannot be arbitrary and should be properly deliberated upon, before they can be put in effect. Administrative officers are quite often required to take on the spot decisions in public interest due to the exigencies of circumstances. In the case of frequently occurring natural calamities and other emergencies, it has become the rule, rather than the exception. These decisions, by its nature will be ad hoc and hence arbitrary, as all the factors required for a 'speaking order' or reasoned decision are unlikely to be available. The analogy for such a situation is often compared to a war like situation and work being taken up on war footing. In fact the analogy is not completely misplaced in cases of natural calamities. However, too frequent use of this comparison, even in routine administrative matters has trivialised it.

The question is whether civil administration has been trained for such war like situations, as the armed forces are trained for war. Training for the armed forces is entirely for war. In the peace time, the forces are trained to be prepared for war and civilian duties are kept at the minimum, not to divert them from their main job. Moreover, the objective in a battle is quite clear, viz. to capture a strategic position with minimum loss to ones own side and maximum loss to the enemy. In fact the objective is made quite clear by the term 'enemy', who has to be fought. In the civilian side, the objectives are much more vague and hence the analogy is hardly appropriate.

In the army in a battle situation, there is a chain of command right down to the lowest level of field formation, i.e. the platoon level. Each functionary is trained for leadership at different level and has to assume full responsibility for the job at hand, which involves putting his life and that of his fellow men at stake. In the civilian side such a situation hardly exists. Lower level civil functionaries, although in most cases are called upon to exercise enormous powers including financial, have neither been trained for any leadership function nor have the same stake, as in battle conditions. He also does not enjoy similar amount of independence or trust of his superiors.

The job is much more complicated, with too many stakeholders in the field. Needs of different individuals and groups are different. The poorer sections will need immediate succour, whereas propertied people will require help in salvaging their property. Similarly, the needs and priority of different individuals will be different. In view of this the task is much more complicated. Decision making system in civilian administrative system is pyramidal with everything emanating from the top. The delegation of responsibility is hardly there. This has the effect of sapping initiative at the lower level, while putting an undue burden on a single functionary like Collector, who is kept busy with ceremonial functions like attending VIP visits. The combination of executive functions with protocol functions considerably curbs the effectiveness of the Collector.

Chapter - X

Way Ahead : Future of Indian Polity

Indian bureaucracy has come a long way since Independence. Expectations from the government have been constantly on the rise and bureaucracy has been the main agency for carrying this programme. In the process, government machinery has considerably extended its reach and has entered into servicing diverse areas as higher education, scientific research, sports, performing arts, etc., besides its normal duties. With such a multifarious clientele, pressure on government services has increased enormously over the years and with it on the bureaucracy. Nobody seems to love the bureaucracy, but there is no getting away from it, as everything depends on government patronage. Over extension of State functions have increased the demand on government services manifold. Such overstretch has created problems, with increased demand from different interest groups. In this clamour for increased demand for public resources, stronger elements have faired much better than the weaker elements.

Although, we have one of the largest technical manpower, educated at State expense, the Indian economy has hardly benefited from the same. In fact, the benefit of this trained manpower has gone mostly to the USA and the UK. This has been a case of aid in the reverse, where a developing country, has subsidised the educational infrastructure of developed countries. Similarly, the State has gone into considerable expenses, since the inception of the plan process for development of scientific knowledge and scientific manpower. But, even after more than fifty years of planning and such huge expenditure, we are dependant on the developed countries for our technological requirements, which constitute a major part of our foreign exchange outflow. There is obviously a serious mismatch between our manpower planning and the requirement of our economy. At the same time, there is no dearth of requirement of foreign consultants, which also constitute a sizeable foreign exchange bill.

This paradox is all the more striking, as the planned development process, was the practical culmination of the rousing words of Jawaharlal Nehru, our first Prime Minister, on the eve of Indian independence. 'The ambition of the greatest man of our generation (Mohandas Karamchand Gandhi) has been to wipe every tear from every eye. That may be beyond us, but as long as there are tears, so long our work will not be over'. The objective of the government was clearly laid down by the leader of the country, which was poverty alleviation and not creating billionaires of international standards. The aim of the first plan was to raise living standards of the people. With that objective in view, it attempted 'the development of human faculties and the building up of an institutional framework adequate to the needs and aspirations of the people'. The aim of development of human capital was to benefit the people of India.

These objectives have hardly been fulfilled, as India contains the single largest population of people below poverty line, in spite of so many years of planning. This has created serious disaffection for the State machinery, leading to a virtual civil war in many parts of the country. Obviously, development process, has bypassed a large section of the people. Why have these objectives enshrined in the ideals of Gandhi and Nehru not been fulfilled? There have been various attempts to find out the reasons for the same. Scapegoats have been found in the form of politicians and bureaucrats. The simplistic answer, which appeals to common sentiment, generally runs like this. Had there been more of selfless politicians in the pre-independence mould and more of bureaucrats with the integrity and efficiency of the ICS officers, things would have been different. This is a pre-independence mindset and does not take into account the changing socio-economic scenario since independence.

Aspirations of individuals for economic and social advancement have skyrocketed and the principle of equity has been the casualty. It has also been suggested that had the economic forces been allowed to operate without political or bureaucratic interference, economic progress would have been better. Some have also blamed the political and bureaucratic corruption for this sorry state of affairs. There is no wishing away the fact that corruption has become a major problem in our polity. We need not necessarily go by the various index of corruption formulated by various Western agencies, whose basic agenda is to show that India and other countries, liberated from the colonial rule, are unable to govern themselves.

The slogan of imperialism that lesser nations are unable to govern themselves, because they are corrupt and lazy, is again raising its ugly head. It must be realised that Colonial countries have yet to reconcile themselves to the loss of colonies, which were the basis for their economic development. An acquisitive capitalist economy is the breeding ground for corruption and with an increase in the money economy, this disease has affected all sections of the society. Political and bureaucratic corruption, cannot take place in a vacuum. It is only possible, when some sections of the society, are partners for the same. The problem of corruption should be looked at in its totality. Prime Minister, Jawaharlal Nehru, when confronted with the problem of corruption in the public distribution system, famously said 'hang the black marketers and hoarders from the nearest lamp post'. Fortunately, this did not start a riot on the ration shops. But the fact remains that even after sixty years of trial and error no better system has evolved and we are dependant on dealers and agents for running our public distribution system. Obviously, they are no paragons of social service. But the public distribution system cannot run without them. Number of social service agencies had taken up management of fair price shops, but all of them had come a cropper. Similarly, we may fervently hate bureaucracy, because it comes into conflict with individualism. But no society can function without rules and there must be bureaucracy in one form or the other to administer these. More we are talking against preponderance of bureaucracy, more we are giving ourselves an over-dose of it.

In our quest for transparency in the government system, we have given ourselves another set of bureaucracy in the form of Information Commissioners and their official paraphernalia. Similarly, there is no dearth of bureaucracy in the wake of economic reforms, in the form of commissions and regulatory bodies. Although, some of them are quasi-judicial in nature, they constitute a huge addition to bureaucracy. They are also free from political control. But, accountability is hardly there. For example, formation of regulatory bodies like Securities Exchange Board of India (SEBI) has hardly reduced the recurrence of major scams in the financial sector at regular intervals. Although, when there are major crimes, police are immediately hauled up and responsibility fixed, this hardly happens in the case of policing of the huge financial sector. These regulatory bodies constitute a third tier of organisation, between bureaucracy and judiciary. This is a new innovation and is designed to free the bureaucracy from Parliamentary control. It has been a common experience worldwide that more open economies have bigger governments.[1] In India too, there has been phenomenal expansion of bureaucracy in the form of various regulatory bodies, commissions and committees. This is a comparatively new phenomenon in the bureaucracy and has broadly remained outside the ambit of public administration, although these bodies are integral parts of the system. A new form of bureaucracy has emerged and will be playing crucial role in the future bureaucratic scheme of things.

There are various bodies with their conflicting agenda, which run at cross purposes. Environmentalists do not like large dams and industries, which are supposed to pollute the environment. But, without the large dams constructed during the first two decades of planning, foodgrains self-sufficiency would not have been possible. Similarly, the massive industrial drive taken up through the public sector, built the basic infrastructure for industrial development, without which India would have been still a backward country. Both these required land acquisition on a large scale and consequent displacement of population; of course with adequate compensation and an opportunity to develop a better life. There was serious opposition from the people affected, as well as from different quarters. But there is no free lunch and the price of development had to be paid, if we wanted it. Had the government not been firm, no economic development would have taken place.

Powerful lobbies, as existing today, had not yet developed at that time and the agitation opposing the development project could be treated as a simple law and order problem. These days such things are hardly possible, as the agitation takes a highly moral tone and is backed by the media and various pressure lobbies, both inside and outside the country. It is hardly possible for all these conflicting interests to converge on a plateau of social equilibrium. Rather, each of these pressure groups, have made the government take care of their agenda, by enacting laws and create another bureaucratic organisation to administer the same. Similarly, industrialists do not like government regulations, but at the same time they depend on government lease to build their industrial estates. They do not rely on the open market to purchase their requirement of land through market mechanism. These are some of the paradoxes, with which the society and government have to deal.

Writing before the French Revolution, Montesquieu wrote 'Men are governed not merely by political power, but by many things: climate, customs, manners; from all of which is derived a general spirit'.[2] Indian customs and manners have never been egalitarian; at best it has been paternalistic and condescending. It would have been a miracle indeed, to achieve the ideals of equity set forth in the Constitution in such a social milieu. The custom of intellectual insularity and aloofness is hardly conducive to attune the general populace to the ideals of the Constitution. An intellectual and philosophical revolution is necessary for ushering in a society based on such ideals. Constitution does not work in a vacuum and envisages a societal mindset to make it workable. Jawaharlal Nehru's concept of a scientific temper is the closest thing for transforming a society with a long history of colonial rule and feudalism.

Development of scientific temper is a prerequisite for making the Constitution workable. Such a situation would require questioning many of the existing value system, which is in fact the basis of many of the non-egalitarian and exploitative practices. However, many of these values are so much ingrained, that even highly educated people find it difficult to question them, let alone break free from their shackles. Nehru's conception of 'scientific temper' was not merely creation of an island of scientific knowledge from which common people feel isolated, but a merger of science and society. This is not merely popularization of science, but educating the people, particularly the youth in scientific and rational thinking, free from blind beliefs. This has hardly happened and the educators and the society did not take up Nehru's cue. Perhaps, the intelligence gap between the highly educated and the common people is not as wide, as is generally assumed. Distrust of the intelligence level of the common man should be anathema in a democracy. 'Those with exceptional gifts are not divinely appointed; for all men are divinely appointed or none; they spring from the common body of the people. I have seen Italian peasants who look the image of Fermi, the great physicist'.[3] One can see it anywhere, in any country under any climate, in one's interaction with common people. This also constitutes the basic tenet of all religions, which to a great extent is responsible for the universal appeal of religion, amongst the great body of people. In that way, there is hardly any conflict between democracy and equality with religion. However, religion as interpreted by various intermediaries with vested interest has many times not lived up to its high ideals and in some cases has become a tool for exploitation. Religious practices have many times degenerated into irrationality and tools of aggrandisation and exploitation and have not lived up to the high ideals of the founders. Similarly, the high ideals enshrined in the Constitution, are by themselves no guarantee of a better society, unless there is a social consciousness for the same.

Present scenario is one of mushrooming of various interest and pressure groups aggressively pushing forward their own agenda, with elected representatives taking a back seat. With a growing distrust of the electoral system and with it of the bureaucracy, there has developed a system of pressure groups. These groups often have international support, mostly from the developed Western countries. Most of these countries have a colonial past and a firm belief that they can govern their ex-colonies better than the locals. These groups have agenda of their own, which may not always coincide with the agenda of the government, which is outlined in the electoral manifesto. Functioning of the government has to a great extent been globalized in the last few decades and the international agencies have a considerable say in our domestic affairs. These agencies claim to be more altruistic than the elected governments and have the backing of international experts, who are supposed to be the last thing in global knowledge and know what is best for us. There is more and more out-sourcing of governance to these expert bodies and persons, who seem to know better than the rest of us.

The eroding confidence in the political system and its adjunct the bureaucracy, particularly amongst a section of the educated class, has resulted in a situation, where the latter seems to have lost faith in electoral democracy. They are of the opinion that the country will be better off, if the experts have greater control over governance. In this scheme of things, the concept of self-governance takes a back-seat and puts a discount on the intelligence and ability of common man to order his day-to-day life. The governance by experts, who are not responsible to the elected representatives, is not a healthy portent in a comparatively new democracy. Experts certainly are not omnipotent and cannot claim monopoly of knowledge. Claims of monopoly of knowledge have seeds of dictatorship. Rule by wise people is not the same thing as self-governance. Expertise, where required, has to be a part of the system and not inducted in an ad hoc manner, according to the market standing of any individual or organization at a particular point of time. Most of these things are products of high dose of publicity.

It is not that the system of experts is not there in the government. Department of Atomic Energy functions as an integral part of the government and could attain international standards, without any foreign collaboration or induction of outside experts, whether Indian or foreign. Homi J Bhaba functioned as the Secretary to the Government of India, Department of Atomic Energy and pioneered India's nuclear capability. Required machinery was purchased from the open market, without any conditionality, which would have been required in any foreign collaboration or in induction of foreign experts. Similarly in the field of space research and missile technology, international standards could be achieved without any external experts. In fact, the end of technical support from the erstwhile Soviet Union from the eighties boosted the Indian space and missile programmes and made it of global standard. It is no accident that missile technology could develop in India, only after it was freed from foreign collaboration. Foreign collaboration and foreign experts are hardly conducive to an independent technological policy.

These are only two examples, where global standards in technology could be achieved by government departments, while working within the government system. Scientists of eminence like Homi Bhabha, Vikram Sarabhai, Raja Ramanna and Homi Sethna worked as Secretaries to the Government and not as Advisors. This is of significance, as former are part of the government system and are accountable, the latter are not. Accountability is the key to the governance in a democracy. Ministers are accountable to the Parliament and Secretaries to them. System of advisors is a comparatively new concept in governance. The government machinery is undergoing a change in which a new pattern of bureaucracy is emerging, with another tier of advisors between ministers and regular bureaucracy. Obviously, the faith in the traditional system of bureaucracy as advisors to government has waned. This is bound to demoralize the service officers, as they are bound to feel that they are not considered knowledgeable enough even after spending a better part of their life on the job. However, the Secretariat pattern of governance, with the Secretaries to government as administrative heads, is very much in existence. The new pattern has increased the size of the government machinery. According to the existing Rules of Business, any proposal emanating from outside the system, whether from the Advisors or Committees, will have to be scrutinized in the Department Secretariat. This is absolutely necessary, as Departmental heads are responsible for government finances, which any proposal will involve.

Need for Poverty Alleviation Schemes

The Indian polity at present is much more non-egalitarian, with visible fragmentations. Equity, which had been envisaged, is not merely taught in schools and colleges, but by the society. Society itself is the greatest institution of learning and one learns more of social norms through interaction with fellow members, than in any academic institution. The seeds of non-egalitarianism, which were already there in the society, have sprouted up in the climate of competition, which has been the hallmark of our development process. Climate of competition breeds selfishness and not cooperation and altruism. In this scenario, bureaucrats, who are very much a part of the society, can hardly be expected to act differently. However, the blame for things gone wrong has been laid at the doors of politicians and bureaucrats, both of whom have lost considerable credibility in the process.

Society is generally worked up about failure of poverty alleviation programmes and is in constant search of scapegoats. When we see poverty all-round with islands of prosperity, our conscience needs to be assuaged and scapegoats are necessary. There was a news-item recently that some villagers had gheraoed the local Tehsil office for failing to provide succour to a poor woman, who died of starvation. This is not an isolated incident. There are numerous cases. Generally, it should be the duty of the community or the neighbours to provide immediate relief to a person in distress and not wait for the government agency to provide relief. Social consciousness has eroded to a great extent in a competitive environment, where 'everybody for himself and devil takes the hindmost'. With the changing social values in the pursuit for modernization with unbridled competition, government will have to take up more and more responsibility for those who fall behind in the rat race.

In such a situation, government agency must step in. It is not possible for a distant government, howsoever well meaning or efficient to take care of such eventualities. There is need for local government, which will be more accessible to the people. The states, where the panchayat machinery has taken roots, generally do not have such problems. States, where the panchayat system is not active, generally have this problem. Nowadays, with local government being given greater importance, such type of problems can be better addressed, without undue dependence on distant government. However, such ad hoc measures have no impact on reduction of absolute poverty.

While policies regarding rural development and poverty alleviation have to be formulated at the Central or state levels, their execution will have to be left to the local bodies to a greater extent. The old colonial concept of long reach of Central or state bureaucracy, will have to give way to an active local bureaucracy. It is necessary to have proper institutional support for rural development and poverty alleviation programmes and the local bodies are the proper institutions for the same. Democracy envisages government at the panchayat or borough level and not merely Parliament or state assemblies at the Central or state levels.

The gap between expectations and performance has created a climate of crisis of confidence. Instead of going deeper into the root cause of the problem, we have been trying to find piecemeal solutions. When the panchayati system faced the teething problems at its inception in the fifties and the sixties, greater reliance was placed on the administrative machinery on the ground that the same could be better controlled from the Central or state level. Panchayati system of government posed as a serious competing agency for both the existing administrative system, as well as the political system. If the system of local governance was to function effectively, there was need for greater devolution of both administrative and financial powers. Although, a blue print for the same was drawn up and statutes were enacted in the earlier stages, the same remained dead letters for non issue of statutory notifications and other administrative bottlenecks like problems of sharing of power between existing state administrative agencies and local bodies.

The development programmes are mostly drawn up by the Central Government and funded by it. Since the Centre has no administrative machinery to administer the same, the projects are executed through the state governments, who have to make financial contribution for the same. In view of this, both these governments are keen on having their administrative personnel, over whom they have control for execution of the same. The Central Government has its personnel in the form of All India Service officers, who are in supervisory control over state government officials. Of course, All India Service officers are under the control of state governments, but the fact of their appointment and training by the Central Government, gives the latter considerable leverage over these officials. The state government has complete control over its officials. It may not be so easy to control the elected representatives of local bodies.

There was a move in the early sixties to place newly recruited IAS officers, after their training as Block Development Officer (BDO), who is the Secretary of the Panchayat Samiti. The exercise was not a practical one, as it created situation of uneasy coexistence between the Chairman of the Panchayat Samiti and the Secretary of the same. The post of BDO involves lot of tight rope walking between official interests and non-official demands and is semi-political in nature. The long training of an IAS officer is to go by the rules and eschew all political pressures. If he is to act according to his training instructions, he is bound to come into conflict with the elected representatives of the Panchayat Samiti, who are supposed to be his official superiors. The position will not be comfortable for the elected members, if the IAS, BDO wants to go strictly according to rules, which he will most likely do, since as a new recruit he will be unlikely to take the risk of bending the rules. The experiment however was soon abandoned.

This is, however, a basic problem in administration, as a rule bound bureaucracy cannot be pro-active and may lack the required dynamism. On the other hand, if rules are interpreted according to the needs of the situation, the official concerned may face administrative problems at a later stage. Unless, there is adequate protection for bona fide decisions taken in administrative interest, this dilemma will persist. There are numerous instances of gung-ho BDOs, who were held up as models of development officers, getting into trouble, when audit pointed out after a long lapse of time that some of the rules have not been strictly followed. After the initial flush of enthusiasm with local self-government as an engine of development, there followed a period, when the elected panchayats were in hibernation. The panchayat system has since been revived, with full statutory backing. Once this system takes firm root in the Indian body polity, democratic apparatus will be further strengthened. In fact, local needs can be better met through proper functioning of local bodies, than by creating more number of states, with a top heavy administrative apparatus.

Another feature in the development of administration during the last several decades has been the steady decline in the role of Secretariat in the decision making process and formulation of government policies. This became more apparent from the seventies. A government elected on a huge popular mandate, with an agenda of its own and in a hurry to implement the same, did not like to be bogged down with long winded notes, discussing the pros and cons of the proposals and their short term, as well as long term implications. This limited the role of the Secretariat considerably and its role became one of processing and communicating government orders.

A conflict between political expediency and bureaucratic norms was brewing. In this political expediency was naturally the winner and bureaucratic norms, also ridiculed as red tapism were side stepped. The officialdom adopted themselves to the new situation with alacrity. The Secretariat of the political executive was strengthened with induction of large number of like minded service officers, who were personally chosen by the former. This Secretariat assumed greater importance than the general Secretariat and all major decisions emanated from it. The problem of red tapism could be solved by inducting number of selected bureaucrats in the political system. These officials enjoyed considerable power and acted as a link with the bureaucratic system. Although this ensured peaceful coexistence between the political executives and the bureaucracy, it made the bureaucracy upward looking. It has also made the system more personalised and affected its objectivity and impartiality. One may not be enamoured of bureaucratic rules and their applications, but the system was designed to ensure transparency and impartiality.

Decision taken in a hurry, because the boss wants the same, may not always be the right decision. The problem of an upward looking bureaucracy is that hardly anybody will like to take decision on his own without consulting his superior, for fear of annoying him. The adage becomes 'boss knows the best'. This stifles independent view and gives way to group view, which is in effect the view of the dominant person in the organisation. This stifles initiative and ability to take independent decision without consulting the boss. Need to take independent decision at every level according to rules, is of utmost importance in the efficient functioning of the government machinery. All decisions are not likely to please everybody. In view of this, an aggrieved party can appeal to a higher functionary. However, people expect quick action from the government system and the process of decision making and action thereon, have to be within a reasonable time frame.

This assumes particular importance, as large amount of public funds are involved in most of these decisions. When large amount of public funds are involved or the decision is of great public importance, due prudence is necessary and it is the duty of professional bureaucracy to point the pros and cons of the matter impartially. This is, however, not to the liking of many, who want quick action. A proper balance between quick action and properly considered action after due examination of the same, has yet to evolve and till such time, the former is the ruling philosophy. This has resulted in some of the projects running into rough weather.

The main role of bureaucracy, as an agency for checks and balances has been considerably reduced. Those who venture to give unsolicited advice are likely to be called negative elements, although later events may prove them right. But people live for the present and nobody is interested in the long run. However, public policy requires statesmanship and long run impact on the polity is no less important than short term gains. Exercise of statesmanship requires organisational support and can better be done through free and frank discussion and not through cronyism. An independent bureaucracy is a safeguard against cronyism. The practice of cronyism and networking has spread fast and bureaucracy has been affected by it.

While the formal role of bureaucracy in policy formulation through the Secretariat mechanism has been reduced, the role of selected bureaucrats in these matters has increased. Such officials act as advisers to the Ministers, either in formal or informal capacities. In that capacity, the line between officials and politicians is blurred and one is likely to step into the area of the other. This leads to a situation, where bureaucrats are as much politicians, as politicians are bureaucrats. With the decline of formal bureaucratic apparatus for policy formulation, there has been growth of different agencies, actively lobbying their own agenda. These organisations have considerable influence on government programmes and policies and often work in tandem with government departments. Heads of these agencies and institutions find place in different committees, constituted by government departments to advice on policy matters.

The position has become one, where the government departments do not have much faith in their own expertise and have to depend on outside experts for their functioning. These organisations, which are outside the government system and are not bound by government rules and regulations, can offer their advice more independently than is possible within the system. However, these bodies, which are not bound by government rules and regulations and are not answerable to the legislature, have no responsibility or accountability for their prescriptions. In fact responsibility is the cardinal principle of the government system in a representative democracy. This practice in fact constitutes outsourcing of government work.

Informal (Parallel) Bureaucracy

A system of informal bureaucracy or parallel bureaucracy has grown over the years. The organisations or institutes or experts, who are called upon to advice the government on various policy matters, mostly constitute of retired academics or officials. Various other powerful lobbies have emerged with their own agenda and have considerable influence on the government policies. There is no doubt that many of them have worthwhile agenda, but some of them are in conflict with each other. For example institutions, which work as think tank for industrial interests, are unlikely to see eye to eye with those sponsoring environmental issues or those espousing labour rights. Most of these bodies have one point agenda, with the brief to push through the same, irrespective of its socio-economic impact. Education on AIDS or sexually transmitted diseases may encourage promiscuity in adolescents, if not properly handled. Similarly, it is a matter of debate, whether AIDS should top the agenda of health care at the cost of primary health facilities for all. Resources being limited, a choice has to be made and the decision has to be political.

To cite an environment related issue, there was pressure on the Chinese government from international environmental lobbies to close down number of industries, which are considered polluting by present day international (western) standards. However, it is these industries, which have contributed largely to China's industrial growth and not the so-called sophisticated industries. It is another issue that these standards are continuously changing to the disadvantage of the countries, which are late entrants in the industrial field. After having achieved industrial development through the so-called polluting industries, the Western countries do not want to lose their advantage.

Closing down these industries would have involved enormous job loss apart from slowing economic growth. There was, however, a counter pressure from the local bodies not to close down these industries, to prevent such job loss. The Chinese government had to take the politically correct decision of allowing these industries to function to prevent enormous job loss and consequent human suffering, which the closure would have involved. Ultimately, all expert advice will have to face the test of political correctness in any system of governance. Unlike the field of experts, where everything can be visualised in terms of black and white, in the management of human affairs, events and situations cannot be interpreted in such simplistic terms. Development of expert knowledge can hardly expect to compete with the complexity of human affairs. For management of human affairs, we have to depend on the politicians, rather than experts.

To evaluate these agenda, sponsored by high profile organisations and persons, government machinery must have their own internal experts. In case, a general bureaucracy needs expert advice and the same is not available internally, it is necessary to have a panel of experts, who work within the government system. Such a panel of experts should be chosen by an autonomous body like the Union Public Service Commission. This will also give necessary transparency to the selection of experts to advice the government. At present these experts inducted from the open market, do not function as civil servants, but exercise lot of power and influence in the government. Persons functioning in the public service must be accountable and bound by the discipline of the system. Their selection should not be on ad hoc basis, but according to the due process. Otherwise 'spoils system',[4] which is against the spirit of the Constitution, may creep in.

While the role of the bureaucracy in 'advising and cautioning the government'[5] (the classic role of civil service, as enunciated by AV Dicey, one of the authorities on the working of the British civil service) has been severely curtailed, the role of bureaucracy in the execution of any government policy remains paramount. Large amount of public funds were allocated since the seventies on various poverty alleviation cum development programmes and the execution of these were entrusted on the administrative machinery. This was a comparatively new role for the latter, but their performance was of utmost importance for the success and credibility of these programmes drawn up at the highest government level. However, the execution level was manned by comparatively junior functionaries, with Collector being the kingpin of the system.

Apart from the altruism involved, these programmes had considerable political importance, with the political executives staking their career and credibility on the results of the same. This got the bureaucracy involved in controversy and as such affected the execution of the same. Since these schemes aimed at creating major structural changes in the society by attempting to empower poorer sections, it naturally involved some amount of social engineering, which is bound to be controversial in attempting to change the existing socio-economic value system. These ambitious government projects at empowerment are not mere administrative exercises, but are major ventures in socio-economic changes. It is also against the existing economic logic, which is based on the model of the existing socio-economic structure. Dependence only on administrative machinery without educating the society on the changing social and economic structure, creates its own problems in that the society is generally reluctant to accept the same. This creates counter pressure in the form of existing power groups trying to garner the greater portion of the benefit of these schemes for themselves. This is the genesis of corruption in the execution of these schemes.

Some attempts have been made since the late nineties to involve the Non-Government Organisations (NGOs). But these organisations have their own agenda, which may not be in consonance with government policies. They are not also bound by government rules and regulations and as such cannot be held accountable. Some of these organisations have international ramifications, which may create conflict of interest with national policies. Experiment of implementing government programme through selected NGOs has hardly been successful and there have been serious complaints of corruption with the added problem of lack of non-accountability. There have been instances of conflict between these bodies and local elected representatives. There are also instances of nexus between some bureaucrats and NGOs, which have led to siphoning of public funds. However, some of these organisations have done commendable work, particularly in the field of environment. The presence of some of these bodies has to some extent acted as catalytic agents and has made the bureaucracy more sensitive to people's need.

Experiment with the NGOs, for executing government work is on the wane. Panchayat system, which has been put in place, can tackle local problems more effectively than a distant bureaucracy or NGOs, however well meaning they may be. The basis of any democratic government is a system of responsibility to the constituents. Elected local self government system is the closest thing, we can have in ensuring responsibility to the constituents. Officials should be responsible to these bodies. It is of urgent importance to develop a system of local level bureaucracy to enable the local bodies to discharge their duties. The NGOs working in the locality should work in coordination with local bodies and ensure there is no conflict of interest. Unless local bodies are given due importance, it will not be possible for them to discharge their duties effectively. Leadership should be nurtured at the local level and there is no better institution for this, than the local bodies. There are likely to be plenty of hiccups in the functioning of these bodies. But with several tiers of governing machinery in place, these could be well rectified and should not provide an alibi for suspension of the system. Democracy to be effective must function at the grass-root level and not merely at the national or state level. This was well understood by the founders of the Constitution.

Distrust of Elected Representatives

A disturbing trend has developed over the years, particularly amongst the educated class that the politicians are responsible for all the ills besetting the society. To many of them, politics has become a dirty word. These people, in view of their positions, are also opinion makers in the society. These views have permeated to the younger generation of professionals, who are market savvy and think the markets can do no wrong. Of course, we are all accustomed to the vagaries of the market and the recent roller coaster ride of the market should have shaken our absolute belief in the market. Distaste for politics and politicians, is a dangerous trend and unless this trend is controlled, it will prove inimical to the continuance of democracy. Distrust of politicians, is lack of faith in the democratic system and ultimately of the common man. This is but expected in a society with a long history of intellectual isolation and elitism, with little faith in the intelligence of common man. It is not that the politicians are the only corrupt element in the society and nor are they the fountainhead of corruption. In today's acquisitive and highly non egalitarian socio-economic scenario, financial corruption is a very much complex phenomenon and not simply a problem of moral turpitude. In this scenario, riding the moral high horse is to say the least presumptuous. We cannot have a democratic polity, without a political system. This requires practitioner of politics (politicians) and political parties, who are indispensable for the functioning of democracy.

Our concept of politician is naive and based on outdated pre-independence concept of freedom fighter, who was prepared to sacrifice himself for independence of the country. Even then, a large scale freedom movement would not have been possible without financial support from nationalist minded persons, whether in business or elsewhere. Politics is a profession and should be treated as such and not as an easy means of achieving power and money. Once, this is lost sight of, politics degenerates. This is to a lesser extent true of the bureaucracy, as well. However, generally one cannot make a foray into bureaucracy at any time, but will have to take it up as a life time profession. In the case of politics, there are lots of lateral entrants, particularly in times of elections.

Democratic politics in its present form is a comparatively new profession in India and is a post-independence development. In a direct electoral system, successful political candidates will have to represent all sections of the population. This brings them in closer contact with sections of population, with whom, the visible upper class and the intellectuals, has hardly any contact or empathy. Although the Constitution provides for a casteless and classless society, this has hardly been possible. In fact, over the years, economic disparity has increased manifold. Elected representatives are to represent the entire cross-section of the society and more of the lower strata, since they constitute the bulk of the electorate. They are, in fact, society in miniature. Criminalisation of politics to a certain extent reflects a greater societal problem. These are some of the fundamental questions, we have to ask ourselves and take remedial steps accordingly.

Democracy, as envisaged in the Constitution, requires equality, to be properly functional. Even in the United Kingdom, on which country's democratic institutions, we have modelled our own to a great extent, a judge was moved to remark in the middle of the twentieth century: "Justice is open to all - like the Grill Room of the Ritz Hotel!"[6] If this was the position in the UK, at the end of two centuries of colonial rule and with a much higher per capita income, the equality scenario in India will certainly be much worse. Framers of the Constitution had visualised a new India, with the crumbling of the caste system, with the empowerment of one individual, one vote. But the things did not work out as visualised. The answer does not lie merely in deterioration of persons at the helm of affairs, as many would like to assume.

Over the years, economic inequality has increased tremendously, creating serious social tensions. This process got accelerated with the economically acclaimed reforms regime initiated since the nineties. International economic competition started from that time might have improved the economic parameters of India. But this has been due to huge transfer of resources from the economically weaker sections to the economically stronger, who are the prime movers in the methodology of development adapted by us[6]. In the existing post-socialistic scenario of the nineties, India could not have avoided certain amount of pro-capitalistic measures, for fear of being left behind in the international rat race.

This pattern of development has not been an unmixed blessing. There has been heavy price to pay in terms of increase in poverty and growing inequality. Although, we have produced number of billionaires through the globalisation process, India ranks very low in human development index and poverty index. (The latest human development report released by UNDP on December 18, 2008, ranks India at 132 in 2006, down four places from the position in 2005). Human Development Index is a much more inclusive and multidimensional indicator of development than GDP (Gross Domestic Product).

Obviously the reforms process has not helped the country in addressing the major problem of poverty alleviation and improving the quality of life of the people. Increased economic inequality has spawned serious social tensions, with urban centres experiencing a population explosion, with limited infrastructure. Visitors from abroad, even from poorer African countries, are aghast at the level of poverty and the great socio-economic disparity in India. From a caste-based society, we are graduating to a class-based society. Increase in violent Naxalite activities in many parts of the country, together with the inability or hesitancy of the State machinery to effectively handle the same, indicate that all is not well in the socio-economic front in many parts of the country. It is also matter of concern that these movements have lot of support from various human rights groups, both within the country and outside, preventing the governments, both Central and state, from taking strong action against them. It is certainly not a simple coincidence that these movements have grown in strength, proportionately with the much acclaimed reforms process.

The situation is one of conflict between political equality and growing economic inequality, which poses a dangerous challenge to the democratic system. In fact, the violent movements of extreme left organisations and their growing strength are manifestations of this conflict situation. This paradoxical situation has also led to the development of various organisations, which have their own agenda. None of these offer any permanent solution. It is of utmost significance to note that the situation has not boiled over, due to the existence of the much maligned political system. Regular election process has provided an opportunity to exercise political equality.

Corruption has crept into the system, partly because of the huge inequality, which is corrupting the socio-economic situation. It is not that democratic system is more corrupt than other systems. It is more apparent, because this is the only open system and the political modus operandi is to criticise each other in public to gain public support. This is also the only system, which depends on public criticism for its sustenance. All other systems are insular and closed systems and are not open to public criticisms.

The corporate governance continues to be a closed system and the reforms process has hardly touched it in ensuring accountability. In India it is also a closely controlled family based organisation. The classic case is the recent Satyam fiasco, where one family with a small percentage of share holding, could criminally siphon of public funds for years together and all concerned pleaded to be blissfully unaware of the same.[7] Regulatory mechanisms, which have been put in place, have been of little help in preventing major scams. In fact, they have been blissfully unaware of the serious illegal activities, which have been going on for years and have come into the picture when the scams have blown up on their own. It is necessary that these regulatory bodies should be fully accountable to the government and the shareholders.

Need for Greater Legislative Control

Since the economic reforms process began in 1992, India has been restructuring its financial architecture, including the regulatory mechanism, largely on the US model. It should be a matter of concern that in the USA, the regulatory mechanism, has completely failed to protect the small shareholders and depositors interest. They have been only championing the cause of major shareholders, on the alibi of preventing further deterioration of the economy. Policy of the guardians of the financial system seems to be one of rewarding wrong doers at the cost of the law abiding majority. This has drawn strong criticism from the legislature, although the executive has remained silent. The Chairman of the Federal Reserve Board had to admit his mistake in advocating and following wrong policies leading to economic crisis, under intense questioning by the legislature committee.

Surfacing of major scandals at regular intervals, particularly in the financial sector, puts a big question mark on corporate governance and the efficacy of the regulatory system. Regulatory bodies are caught in the dilemma of non interference in corporate matters and safeguarding public interest. They seem to have preferred the former, as this is the dominant economic logic of liberalisation. Present economic slowdown has highlighted some of the maladies in the corporate sector, both within the country and outside. These are only tips of icebergs and the system of accountability continues to be more or less non existent. This in spite of the fact that corporate sector is heavily dependent on public funds for its functioning. Corporate governance can be only successful, if there is an organised alert body of small shareholders and depositors. This, however, is unlikely in the present scenario. It is necessary to have an active and prompt grievance machinery to address the complaint of small shareholders and depositors. Since the corporate sector functions largely on public funds, there should be no difficulty in introducing Right to Information Act, as far as the management of public funds is concerned.

The professional bodies have their own system of management and are not answerable to the public or any external agency. They constitute intellectual organisations, which are beyond the purview of average citizen. However, these bodies have considerable influence in public life and also act as advisers to elected governments, which have considerable faith on them, due to their intellectual aura. Moreover, higher education being highly subsidised, these organisations are also to a great extent publicly funded and to some extent should be publicly accountable. Knowledge groups, which claim absolute wisdom in their sphere, may become another new class, unless they submit themselves to a social audit. This will be only possible, if their work is discussed in independent fora. Parliamentary control over all such bodies, which are publicly funded, is essential in a democratic polity.

In the United States, various empowered committees of the Legislature keep a close watch on the functioning of publicly funded bodies. In the wake of various corporate scandals in the nineties, in which major audit and accountancy firms were involved, the US legislature passed the Sarbanes-Oxley Act in July, 2002 by near unanimity, against stiff opposition from the business lobby. This Act brought major changes in the accounting and audit methodologies and made the audit firms more accountable. Similarly, the US legislative committee, while probing into the economic down turn, was not impressed by the polemics of experts and made them accountable for their wrong economic policies, which cost the nation dearly. All these professional bodies represent the forces of Establishment. In that way, bureaucracy is also an integral part of the Establishment.

Need for Democratising the Bureaucracy

Role of a professional bureaucracy in a democratic system has to be one of supporting the system and not have an independent agenda of their own. Loyalty should be to the Constitution and national welfare and not to any personality. Personal based loyalty is not in consonance with a democratic polity and is more suited to a system of courtiers than a democratic system. In our system, political executives are subject change through the ballot, but bureaucrats have an unhindered tenure. This has been designed for the continuance of the system. This, however, puts the bureaucrats in an advantageous position vis-à-vis the political executives, which are sometimes countered by large scale transfer of officialdom. Of late there has been a tendency towards 'spoils system' by bringing in associates in the form of advisors. This has to a great extent reduced the importance of regular bureaucracy. It has also led the bureaucracy being politically savvy.

A successful bureaucrat cannot afford to be insular and must develop lot of right contacts, which is the key to a successful career. This does not, however, encourage the creation of a professional bureaucratic organization, but one that plays to the gallery and is more publicity oriented than work ethics oriented. Uncertainty at the political level has also been transferred to the bureaucracy, particularly regarding tenure.

The common concept of public administration is one of generalist bureaucracy and not of various other government functionaries, who constitute a sizeable portion of the government system and are much larger in number. This is to a great extent due to the high visibility of the generalist system in administration. As we have analysed earlier, political executives being generalist themselves, find it convenient to work with generalist officials, rather than deal directly with technical personnel. In fact, the generalist bureaucracy acts as a buffer between the political executives and the specialist cadres. This makes it the most visible part of the system and also an important power group. It is also the main instrument of administration for the political elite. This also leads to politicisation of bureaucracy.

The bureaucratic system was devised to ensure continuance and to ensure that there is no disruption in governance with change of political executives. However, tenure of higher officials, being on an average much shorter than the political executives, this premise does not hold good. As has been discussed, there has been increased tendency to depend on advisers and commissions for major decisions. Thus there has been a tendency to bypass the usual bureaucratic process. These developments, together with the need to set up administrative reforms commissions at regular intervals, show that confidence in the existing administrative system has considerably waned. Uncertainty of tenure has also eroded the morale of officialdom, particularly at the higher level.

Latest report of the Administrative Reforms Commission suggests periodic reviews to discontinue with the services of officials found unsuitable. This is designed to increase the efficiency of civil service officials and bring public administration at par with the private sector. Obviously, it is presumed that the latter system is more efficient than the former, in spite of the fact that government service in India attracts lot of talented people, who are rigorously selected. The Commission has zeroed in on the fact that continuity of service and the absence of a system of hire and fire is the main cause of inefficiency in government system. It has been recommended that a new clause should be provided at the time of appointment that continuity of service would depend on periodic review of performance. Fear of punishment seems to be the most popular method of reforming the bureaucracy.

According to all the available psychological evidence, fear is not a desirable emotion in an individual and modern management theories have scrupulously eschewed this emotion as a motivating factor. It is an outdated concept that fear is the best of the motivating factors for an individual. Syndrome of fear perverts the mind of an individual and we cannot afford to have a bureaucracy motivated by fear in a democratic polity. It can be argued that only the inefficient have reasons to fear. But who decides whether an official is inefficient. It is at best a subjective judgment of one individual about another. All round the year assessment and review will create a situation, where officials will only be interested in impressing their official superiors. This will create an Orwellian situation in bureaucracy, which is already an insular system. It is necessary to have a closer look at the functioning of the system itself. Indispensability of some officials, even beyond retirement and quick turn over of bulk of the officials, even before they are able to settle down on their jobs, should be matter of concern. Are we going in for a patronage bureaucracy?

There are circles within circles in the power structure, which is basically a closed system. This is to a great extent reflected in the functioning of the Parliament and the State legislatures. The Parliamentarians have to frequently resort to agitational methods to air their views in the Parliament, instead of the procedural method. Even the Speaker of the last Lok Sabha, a veteran Parliamentarian and an eminent Jurist, condemned such behaviour in very strong language. Agitations inside the Parliament had drawn condemnation from the Press. While it is easy to condemn this, the problem lies deeper. It is unlikely that the legislators, who are representing millions of people, are indulging in mass irrationalism to press their problems, before the executive wing of the government, which is their creation. More probable reason seems to be that the legislative wing is feeling alienated and excluded from the power structure and is left with no other alternative than resorting to agitational methods. If this is the case, there is certainly necessity of democratising the power structure. To begin with, there is need of greater involvement of the legislative wing in the power structure.

The basic problem is, whether a few undesirable individuals are corrupting the system or the system itself has developed some flaws. Any system develops through a process of gradual evolution and cannot simply be ordered from above. It is necessary to find out whether the present bureaucratic system is allowing the development of individual talents or otherwise. Fear psychosis is not the best of motivating factors. In fact, it may prove to be positively dangerous in a democratic polity. A bureaucratic system which manages its internal administration on dictatorial tenets will certainly transmit these tenets to the society at large. Bureaucratic efficiency cannot be at the cost of democratic values. A person, who is a progeny of a dictatorial system, will find it difficult to administer a democratic system. Such a person will be effective in a dictatorial system. These are some of the vital facts, which we have to keep in mind while thinking of restructuring the bureaucratic system.

The main reason of attraction for government service is the continuity of tenure. In fact, this is one of the principle reasons, which attract lot of bright young persons to the public service with comparatively lower emoluments. Once one enters government service, one surrenders considerable amount of rights as a private citizen, which is not the case in other sphere of activities. It should be of interest to analyse, why persons, who have been recruited through an open system, are unable to deliver the results according to public expectations. Whether the defect lies in undesirable persons, who have managed to enter the system and have corrupted the system or the problem lies in the system itself? It is unlikely that a few individuals are corrupting the system and getting rid of them will solve the problem. As it is, bureaucracy has a system of dealing with inconvenient individuals. There are number of low priority posts, where such individuals can be placed, without going through the rigmarole of due process of law. This in fact constitutes a sort of bureaucratic purgatory. Solution to the bureaucratic malaise lies in democratising the system. A system, which depends on fear as a motivating force for its efficiency and sustenance, will degenerate into a dictatorial one. If the bureaucracy becomes a dictatorial entity, it is hardly in consonance with a democratic polity. In fact, if the bureaucracy is democratised in its functioning, individual talents will flourish and efficiency will increase.

Endnotes

1. Dani Rodrik, *Globalization and Labour, in Market Integration, Regionalism and the Global Economy* (1999), Edited by Richard Baldwin, p.142, Cambridge University Press.
2. Edward Gibbon, *The Decline and Fall of the Roman Empire* (Vol.1, p.lx), Everyman's Library (1993).
3. Herman Finer, *The Theory and Practice of Modern Government* (1962), p. 952, Methuen & Co. Ltd. London.
4. The Spoils System is generally attributed to President Andrew Jackson (1829) of the United States. Under the Spoils System, the party winning the election makes gifts of government jobs to its favourites.
5. AV Dicey, *Law of the Constitution.*
6. Frederic A Ogg and Harold Zink, *Modern Foreign Governments,* (1957), p. 356, The Macmillian Company, New York
7. Subramanian Swamy, *Corruption and Corporate Governance in India* (2009), Har-Anand Publications Pvt. Ltd.

Index

Notes

Notes